George Edgerly Harris III
date unknown, Harris family archives

How This Book Came To Be

A LIFE Magazine Specialty Edition hit newsstands on September 5, 2014. It is titled, "The Vietnam Wars / 50 Years Ago - Two Countries Torn Apart." The cover contrasts two photographs from 1967: a battlefield image by David Douglas Duncan, and "Flower Power" by Bernie Boston, depicting a young man answering the brandished gun barrels of armed soldiers with gentle flowers at a Pentagon anti-war demonstration.

The enduring image of the brave, peace-loving teenager in a turtleneck sweater, placing flowers into the soldiers' gun barrels, went far beyond being a runner-up for the Pulitzer Prize. Over time this iconic moment made "Flower Power" the most powerful anti-war catchphrase of the 1960s. But the big idea represented by this image is not just about one person or one moment in time.

As America struggles to find its way in 2017, Bernie Boston's photograph is a timely reminder of the pressure and contention arising from opposing systems of belief, then and now: war and peace. This clash of irreconcilable views continues to fuel the ongoing societal struggle in America and around the world.

Flower Power Man is the culmination of inspiring events in the counter-culture of the 1960s and 70s. As Bernie Boston's historic photograph celebrates its 50th anniversary, and the daily drone of saber-rattling threatens world peace, the authors feel the time is right to share their brother's story by answering the question, **Who was that brave young man demonstrating "Flower Power"?**

Table of Contents

Essay Contributors
in order of appearance

Pam Tent (Sweet Pam)
Kembrew McLeod
Walter Michael Harris
Robert Heide
Claudia Tedesco-Colmer
Susan Dale Rose
Ann Harris
Mark Thompson
Robert Altman
Tahara (James Windsor)
Hibiscus (George Harris III)
Jim Jet (James Tressler)
Adrian Milton
Martin Worman
Robert Croonquist
Lendon Sadler
Andrew Blauvelt
Fayette Hauser
HRH Lee Mentley
Michael Varrati
Rumi Missabu
David Talbot
Do Lee
William Frothingham
John Edward Heys
Tim Robbins
David Loehr
Ilka Scobie
Shelley Valfer
Andrew Sherwood
François Weyergans
Agosto Machado
Angel Jack (Jack Coe)
Daniel Nicoletta
Laurence Frommer
Don Marino
Lance Loud

Paul Zone
Geretta
Penny Arcade
Holly Woodlawn
Michael Musto
Denise Ryan
George Harris, Sr.
Kenneth Ansloan
Laurence Gartel
Timothy Bellavia
Michael Cepress
Carol Dean
Bobby Reed

Photo Contributors
in alphabetical order

Robert Altman
Sheyla Baykal
Bernie Boston / RIT Archives
Dagmar
Fayette Hauser
Joshua Freiwald
Estate of Clay Geerdes
Ingeborg Gerdes
James D. Gossage
Peter Hujar
Michael Ian
Estate of Bud Lee
David Loehr
Mary Ellen Mark
Dan Nicoletta
Gregory Pickup
Chuck Roche
Andrew Sherwood
Bill Weber
David Weissman
David Wise

Dedications

We dedicate this book to Bernie Boston, the photographer who captured the image that best represents Allen Ginsberg's powerful and effective method of peaceful protest … ***Flower Power!***

And to our brother, George E. Harris III, aka Hibiscus, the brave, peace-loving teenager demonstrating at the Pentagon, gently placing flowers into soldiers' guns at the 1967 anti-war demonstration.

We also dedicate this book to Ann Marie McCanless Harris, our amazing mother and Hibiscus' lifelong collaborator and champion. She passed away peacefully on September 10, 2016 during the writing of this book. Ann's total acceptance of her gay eldest child gave him the confidence to address complex social issues in ways that will reverberate in many hearts and in the culture for years to come.

Finally, we dedicate this book to the LGBTQ communities and to programs around the world that support them. They are jewels in the heart of our human family. We are honored to be a part of their history, culture, recognition, acceptance and ever-expanding future.

We hope that *Flower Power Man* will encourage people everywhere and empower their blossoming personalities, talents, courage, ideas and dreams.

Foreword by
Pam Tent

Author of *Midnight at the Palace:*
My Life as a Fabulous Cockette

 I was 19 and homeless when I met Hibiscus. It was an early morning in Golden Gate Park and I heard a voice, singing, through the foliage. Up in a tree, was a dancing apparition of flowing robes and lipstick with a mane of golden hair. He asked me to join him. It was to be a wonderful change of fortune. In the late afternoon sun, I followed this charismatic creature to his home at the Kaliflower Commune and joined the assortment of beautiful saints and sinners that he culled during his travels.

The energy Hibiscus emanated could not be contained just swirling through the streets or dancing in the park. He needed a larger stage, and the Palace Theatre became his Cinema du Paradis where he created lavish musical sequences and a marvelous chaos that lifted the entire audience on his wings.

He had a dream book pasted together of rhinestones and glittered images that he pored through in advance of writing every show. Turning the pages, he would squeal with newfound excitement as if it were his first glimpse of the almost sacred images – then he would recreate his fantasy for the stage. Spontaneity was paramount (much to the chagrin of a few perfectionists in the group) as his whimsy guided his scripting – an homage to a glamour goddess or a more ethereal essence. He was totally in the moment and he glowed.

I lost myself in this wonderful madness and knew I'd found a home. Hibiscus had nicknames for each of us and he sometimes called me "Sister Theresa" and gave me a bracelet with her image. Everywhere he gathered tulle and trinkets – and flowers from the waste bins behind the flower market. And he lived each day in celebration of life, sprinkling his blessings on everyone in his path.

When The Cockettes surprisingly became an underground sensation there were rifts within the ranks. Hibiscus moved on to his real love, free theater and the Angels of Light. I performed with them a few times and eventually Hibiscus and Jack traveled home to New York. The Cockettes continued for a while, as did The Angels of Light, but no one can tell you that things were ever the same. He left us with handfuls of fairy dust but he took the magic with him.

When I started my book about the irascible Cockette family, Scrumbly advised me: "Be kind. Just remember that Hibiscus found something in each of us to love." We were all hand-chosen and in retrospect, I have no idea where I would have gone that day. But I met Hibiscus, and he showed me the way.

Introduction

 George Harris III was a key member of what I refer to as the "downtown diaspora" in *The Pop Underground*, a forthcoming book to be published by Abrams in fall 2018. My book traces the ways the denizens of the downtown reshaped social life far beyond the relatively small one square mile area of Lower Manhattan. One example of this is the way that Hibiscus was famously photographed at an October 21, 1967 antiwar rally in Washington, D.C., placing flowers in the rifles of National Guardsmen who lined the perimeter of the Pentagon. His theatrical flourish became a powerful metaphor for peaceful nonviolent resistance, pushing the term "flower power" to the forefront of the national imagination. Two years later, George founded The Cockettes in San Francisco and reinvented himself as Hibiscus, then moved back to New York to rejoin his amazing sisters and mother in the Angels of Light. He was like a psychedelic Joanie Appleseed who spread his visionary, gender-fluid performance style from coast to coast, from New York to San Francisco to Europe and back again. Through his embodied performances of a wide range of sexualities, he helped set the gay and trans revolution in motion.

This is one of the primary reasons why I chose Hibiscus as one of my book's main characters. I chose to spotlight him along with other lesser-known figures like Ellen Stewart and Harry Koutoukas to hopefully introduce them to a wider audience. While Hibiscus was not as famous as some of *The Pop Underground's* other main characters – such as Andy Warhol, Patti Smith, and Debbie Harry – his impact on the arts and our wider culture was just as profound.

One of the great privileges of writing *The Pop Underground* was getting to know many of my interview subjects (I conducted about 150 interviews, totaling well over one million words of transcripts). The Harris family's collective warmth, openness, creativity, and bravery deeply moved me the more I dug into their history; Hibiscus lives on thanks to their love and passion.

Kembrew McLeod
Professor of Communication Studies
University of Iowa

10

PART I - THE EARLY YEARS

***Hibiscus was captivated with Peter Pan and Never Never Land at an
early age. He wholeheartedly embarked on a lifelong journey of
theatrical magic and enchantment.***

Peter Pan *written by J. M. Barrie*
The song Never Never Land,
music bu Jule Styne, lyrics by Betty Comden and Adolph Green (1)

Chapter 1
Postwar Euphoria

George Edgerly Harris III
was born on September 6, 1949.
He came into the world as the
Grand Marshall of the Parade!

In the sleepy little Norman Rockwell-style town of Bronxville, New York, George Edgerly Harris Sr. and Ann Marie McCanless Harris brought a beautiful, spirited boy into the world and named him George Edgerly Harris III after his father and grandfather. Their young family was entertained by *Your Hit Parade* on the radio, *Howdy Doody* on TV, and embraced the hope of a nation of citizens who were recovering from the disruption and cruelty of World War II.

This postwar euphoria arose from the promise of American prosperity on the horizon. Many couples decided this was the ideal time to begin a family. The Servicemen's Readjustment Act of 1944, known informally as the G.I. Bill, provided low-cost mortgages, college tuition and one year of unemployment benefits to returning veterans. (2)

George Harris, Sr. (left) and Ann Marie Harris (right), holding their daughter, Jayne Anne. Photos by Ruth SoRelle.

Now a war veteran, George Sr. was the son and grandson of fine art painters George Edgerly Harris and Charles Xavier Harris. His wife, Ann Marie McCanless, was the daughter of a successful Westchester oral surgeon and a spirited Irish homemaker.

As newlyweds, George and Ann settled in Bronxville, a short commute from New York City. They embraced the suburban American dream of the 1950s: a house with lovely furniture, a new car and children. Over the next twelve years, young George III's siblings Walter Michael, Frederic Joseph, Jayne Anne, Eloise Alice and Mary Lucile Harris were born, in that order.

The Harris children were raised on the Catholic Church, Cub Scouts and Brownies, Mickey Mouse Club, and lively beer-barrel piano music provided by their Irish aunt Ella, who they called Yaya. Favorite records from the Swing Era and musical theater played round the clock.

Ann and George played bridge with their Westchester friends and raised their family as society expected.

Young George's curiosity about people and resonance with flower power were evident even then. At the age of three he unlatched the white picket fence and wandered off to explore the world outside the gate. After several nail-biting hours the toddler found his way home and presented a tattered bouquet of chrysanthemums to his panicked mother. Neither upset, afraid nor desperate to be back at home, little George joyfully described the streets of Bronxville, the people he had seen, what they were wearing and his delight at coming home to tell his mother "all about it," a recurring theme throughout his life. George Harris III would forever have a special bond with his adoring mother, Ann.

George III's 8th birthday party in Bronxville, NY, 1957

In 1958, when George was nine years old, his family longed for more than Bronxville had to offer. They pulled up deep-rooted stakes and said goodbye to Norman Rockwell. The Harris family moved – lock, stock and barrel – to Clearwater Beach, Florida, where blue oceans and white beach sands replaced the grey mundane boredom that was suburbia.

School photo, age 10, in Clearwater, Florida, 1959

George III, nicknamed "G3," was a driven boy who from childhood wanted to make a name for himself. He thrived on attention and was determined to be an actor.

He spent much of his boyhood studying theater, writing his own scripts, and casting friends, family and neighbors as performers while signing up others to create choreography and build sets and costumes of his own design. After much study with the Clearwater Little Theater Junior Workshop, where he was declared by director John Mayo to have leadership qualities, young George began to write his own adaptations of Shakespeare and Broadway shows. He enlisted his family members to write songs, play a variety of characters, and drum up audiences, efforts that drew the attention of local newspapers.

The Junior Workshop provided the most well rounded training that kids in theater could hope for. It was young George, responding to a newspaper ad that got his family involved – first, his siblings, then his mom and dad. As a family they learned the fundamentals of acting, directing, writing, lighting and set design, and producing.

Following his performance as a Witch in Shakespeare's *Macbeth*, eleven-year-old George received this evaluation from workshop director Mayo:

- Mental Attitude: Sincere and co-operative
- Emotional Attitude: High strung but determined
- Social Attitude: Shy, but has great popularity

For "General Comments" Mayo wrote:

> "George is unique. By sheer hard work alone, he has mastered the terrific emotional tension he encounters onstage, which adds to the electrifying performance he gives."

With this level of training and encouragement, and total support from his family, George believed he could do anything he wanted in the arts just by having an idea, hatching a plan and rallying the troops.

And so, George Harris III's artistic journey of creating shows, movies and parades as fast as he could think them up, began in those early days near the lapping ocean waves of Clearwater Beach, Florida. His brother, Walter Michael, recalls:

> He viewed the world through myth-colored glasses. Upon landing on Eldorado Avenue in Clearwater, eight-year-old George mused that we (the entire family) had arrived in the fabulous land of Inca gold, Spanish conquistadors and Voltaire's *Candide* - the Land of El Dorado. He read about the legend of a king who covered himself with gold dust before jumping into a lake as part of a ritual. The name "El Dorado" translates literally as "the golden one." He dubbed us all "The El Dorado Players." He absorbed his surroundings and incorporated them into his art, from the palm trees and flamingos of Florida and mythology learned in grade school to the social archetypes he would later poke fun at. (3)

The Harris family's new theatrical troupe consisted of its founder, "G3," his parents, his five brothers and sisters, and many neighborhood children. By Clearwater standards, George had already made theatrical history. He was a tireless theatrical producer. During the El Dorado Players' first season in the summer of 1962, the young producer put on two musical plays written by his mother Ann, *Bluebeard* and *The Sheep and the Cheapskate.* Instant success, at least in the neighborhood, spurred George to adapt, produce, direct, design and star in whatever material was at hand.

When the Richard Burton-Elizabeth Taylor movie *Cleopatra* opened in the local theater, George came up with his own epic version, *Cleopatra, the Nile Queen.* He wrote, produced and directed the play, executed the lavish sets and acted the part of Mark Antony. George liked to cast himself in the starring roles. He quickly followed up with his adaptation of the hit Lerner and Loewe Broadway musical, *Camelot.*

Young George and his all-youngster troupe,
The El Dorado Players, in their adaptation of the Broadway
musical Camelot, *in Clearwater, Florida, 1962*

Local newspapers enthusiastically gave George and the El Dorado Players visibility and plenty of positive reinforcement with reviews and photos. Between these successes, George and his troupe filled in with parades on holidays, a front-yard carnival, and even a casino with a working slot machine, thanks to his father's ingenuity with tools.

George, inspired by his mother's tales of the Titanic, produced and directed a thirty-minute movie, *The Unsinkable Titanic,* with a cast of fifty performers (announcing his penchant for Busby Berkeley style vignettes). No expense was spared on the premiere, the "event of the century," including a rented Klieg light to illuminate the night sky.

The Clearwater, Florida press loved George's theatrical productions. From *The Clearwater Sun*, October 19, 1962:

'Unsinkable Titanic' Triumph
by Beverly Hutchins

George Harris Jr., 13 year-old producer of new plays, outdid himself in his debut as a film director Saturday night with the premiere showing of "The Unsinkable Titanic." The movie began with panoramic shots of elaborate staterooms, the first class ballroom and elite passengers enjoying various activities unaware of the impending tragedy. Included in the unfolding plot were the first signs of concern on the bridge, valiant efforts of the stokers in the boiler room endeavoring to remain at their duties, the perspiring wireless operator frantically jabbing the code key with pleas for help, and the sudden realization and ultimate panic of the passengers. Most realistic and exciting were scenes in the lifeboats when passengers, foundering in the water were hauled aboard to safety. A gripping shot was that of the "dead" captain of the ship floating in the water. The final scene showed the watery grave of the Titanic. Asked if he would like to continue his filmmaking hobby into adulthood, George said "Yeah, but I'd rather do live dramas than make movies … it's a whole lot easier." (4)

With these successes under his belt, George had established himself as a writer, director, producer, performer and leader. The triple threat theater artist and his talented family found themselves yearning for bigger stages and audiences, brighter lights and better opportunities.

Another driver of the decision to leave Florida was George Sr.'s struggle to earn enough to sustain his large family. He knew he could do better in New York City. In addition, Ann harbored concerns about safety for G3 due to his emerging sexual orientation. Ann, who had close gay male friends, had a sixth sense about her precocious son being flamboyant, artistic, gay and gender bending, as he often changed the sex of his sisters' Littlechap dolls. She remembered being deeply concerned over newspaper reports of Tampa police breaking down doors in an effort to catch gay men in "the act." Although Florida did not have a specific sodomy law, the state had an "unnatural and lascivious act" law, which qualified as a second-degree misdemeanor. (5) For these reasons, and the fact that she had lived in and loved New York City, Ann's instincts told her it was time to get the family "outta Dodge."

Walter Michael Harris

G3 and his brother, Walter Michael, in Bronxville, 1955

G3 and Me

Early childhood memories are difficult for me to remember, let alone articulate. At best, I recall an image here, an impression there. But it's clear that my older brother was ever present from Day One.

George was my first friend. My formative years were also his. Our parents had recently lived through World War II and wanted a family, loved children and showered us with positivity and enthusiasm for

19

our wellbeing. Mom's widowed aunt, the irrepressible Ella Driscoll O'Connor, lived with us. She was an excellent cook and baker, played the piano and loved us kids.

G3 and I played together, slept in the same room and wore each other's clothes. His friends were also mine in "our little gang," as Mom liked to say. We enjoyed the atmosphere of America at peace: family meals around the dining room table, school and friends within walking distance, Cub Scout meetings and church on Sunday. We were in Sunday school together with the old-school Catholic nuns. One memorable sign of continuity – George and I had the same first-grade teacher that Mom had had as a young girl.

We made our own fun, with suggestions and practical help from Mom and Dad. Our family loved road trips and took vacations together every summer. We learned how to swim and fish. We visited relatives who had cousins our age that we could play with. As a family we celebrated the Fourth of July, Halloween, Thanksgiving, Christmas and birthdays with traditional touches and homemade decorations.

Although we received store-bought gifts on birthdays and on Christmas morning, our parents modeled a "do-it-yourself" sensibility. What I remember best is Dad's passion for, and skill in, building *things that work*, whether it was a soapbox derby racer for George to drive or a motor-driven model of our solar system for my Science Fair entry in which each planet revolved around the "sun" – a yellow ping-pong ball spinning nine "planets" on a motor at their relative speeds.

One spring Mom turned our revolving backyard clothesline into a Maypole, festooned with brightly colored ribbons. From a back porch phonograph she broadcast a dance tune loudly until, one by one, neighborhood children materialized, each taking up a ribbon and joining in the dance. The magical effect of Mom's initiative was not lost on G3 and me.

George and I agonized together when the family suffered the sudden loss of a third child, a sister, at three months of age, named Ann Marie after Mom. The baby girl was perfectly healthy, so her death was a mystery. We felt our parents' intense grief and tried to understand why. Not even the doctors could answer that question. It happened again just before the family moved to Florida in 1958, a baby brother who never made it home from the hospital.
I was now about six years old and remember asking Dad why, and contemplating life and death for the first time.

George was a natural-born leader of the pack. He was always out front, organizing our gang around some new adventure or other. He depended on my help and I was happy to give it, because he was just plain fun to be around.

G3 was out front in other ways. When Dad and Mom decided to move our growing family to Florida, George went ahead with Dad to scout the scene and find us a place to live. We settled in Clearwater, a sleepy tourist town near Tampa, where Dad had been stationed during the war. Although it was hot and humid in summer, we loved the proximity to beautiful beaches on the Gulf of Mexico. We didn't care for the mosquitos, lizards and big bugs, but loved the tropical flora and fauna: palm trees, orange groves, aloe and thousands of flowers in brilliant colors, including the ubiquitous hibiscus.

Like Bronxville, Clearwater was expanding rapidly with the growing horde of Baby Boomers. G3 and I soon had a new gang of friends and new social circles to travel in. We joined the Youth Center Pram Fleet to learn the rudiments of sailing.

Although it was not his thing, George did learn how to navigate a small fragile craft on an open bay, driven by the wind.

A huge turning point for us was joining the Francis Wilson Playhouse Junior Workshop, a program of our local Little Theater. Signing up was George's idea when he saw their ad in a newspaper. John Mayo was its director, and the best theater teacher a kid could have. Although acting was the main lesson, Mayo insisted that his young actors learn every aspect of stagecraft: directing, set design and construction, lighting, makeup, choreography, improvisation, stage movement, even front and back of house. By this time our siblings, Jayne Anne and Fred, were old enough to participate, and our parents joined in as actors in the adult division.

G3 and I made new theater friends quickly. One of them, Gaylord "Scotty" Church, lived in our neighborhood with his mother and little brother in a large house with a huge yard next to a convent of cloistered Catholic nuns. Scotty's mom loved having us over to play. On summer weekends she would drive us four kids in her gleaming white air-conditioned Cadillac to an exclusive yacht club for lunch and a then a swim in the Olympic-sized pool. For G3 and me it was our first brush with an upper-crust family of means. George noted the class distinction. We were mystified by the watercress sandwiches.

George, Scotty and I made our theater debut at the Junior Workshop playing the Three Witches in *Macbeth*. It was fun to cross-dress, act spooky and speak Elizabethan English. Mayo believed that kids could pull off Shakespeare with little or no modification – and he was right. The Clearwater Little Theater inspired George and Mom to start The El Dorado Players company with our family as the core. This launched a three-year period in which G3 led us all from one home grown production to another and laid the groundwork for our move to New York City to pursue show business for real.

22

The close bond that George and I forged in Bronxville and in Florida stood the test of time. It also withstood the occasional brotherly blow-up, usually a result of his incessant teasing, which I returned in kind. Although our paths diverged as we matured and came into our own, the deep water of our mutual affection endured. We stayed in touch, collaborated when possible, and knew we could count on each other.

Always together, brothers G3 and Walter Michael were poised and determined to replicate their successful El Dorado Players model at the Café La MaMa in New York City.
Photos by James D. Gossage, 1966

23

Chapter 2
New York City
a family reinvents itself off-off-Broadway

November 1964 - Shaking off suburbia, the Harris family departed Florida and headed north in hopes of finding a new environment that embraced freedom of expression and experimental artistry. Photo by George Harris Sr. in Rockefeller Center, NYC

A lot was riding on the move from Clearwater to the East Village of New York City. The family was living "on fumes" as far as money was concerned. Their driving goal was the possibility of real careers as artists and George Sr. wanted to make it all possible. In 1962-63 he undertook an advance scouting trip to New York City to assess work and housing conditions. He discovered a world that newcomer theatrical artists can only dream of, the East Village.

This birthplace of off-off Broadway was a Mecca for anyone with a dream and tenacious grit. A bohemian at heart, the place won George over the minute he set foot on the pavement. Lady Luck was with him in the person of Ellen Stewart, founder of La MaMa Experimental Theater Club, a kindred spirit who helped him find work, housing and resume-building opportunities in his new chosen field.

Ellen Stewart taking one of many bows at her Café La Mama in 1965.
Photo by James D. Gossage

Ellen introduced Dad to Joe Cino, Al Carmines, Lanford Wilson and other rising stars in the off-off-Broadway world. She put him to work straightaway as an actor and director, and was delighted that he was preparing to move his family up from Florida to join the party.

George Sr. had no trouble finding the kind of day jobs that afford theater people the flexible schedules they need. He traveled back to Clearwater and described to the family what he found in New York. They agreed that the next step was to bring G3 to the City to see if he could get a foothold in theater too, and he did. Next, G3 returned to Florida to fetch Jayne Anne, and soon the rest of the family followed. Ellen Stewart wasted no time convincing a skeptical landlord to rent to this enterprising family of eight.

Their new neighborhood at Second Avenue and East Ninth Street was predominantly a Ukrainian settlement. Historically, Second Avenue below 14th Street was home to former venues of the old Yiddish Theater. When the Harris family arrived they found public schools, grocery stores and laundromats within walking distance. In addition, they were in close proximity to the Veselka Diner, the Fillmore East, Ratner's Kosher Deli, Café La MaMa, Caffe Cino, Judson Poets Theater, the Anderson Theater, Hell's Angels, the Hare Krishna temple, St. Marks Place, beatniks and Beats like Allen Ginsberg, Ed Sanders' Peace Eye Bookstore, Andy Warhol's Factory, and The Electric Circus, a Polish ballroom turned psychedelic discotheque.

25

Experimentation in the arts at this time birthed new influences in theater, film, fine art, music, dance, journalism and fashion – and New York's "East Village" seemed to be the nucleus for much of it. The Harris family, with their Westchester roots and theatrical success in Florida, felt like they had landed "somewhere over the rainbow."

Farewell to the gentle sound of beach waves. Hello to police sirens, loud neighbors, garbage trucks, construction clatter and taxi drivers leaning on their horns. Winos slept in their hallway and a gang of glue sniffers held their weekly meeting there. The rooftop made the open sky available if you didn't mind the four flights of stairs. This intense paradigm shift cracked open and expanded young George's creative instincts. They were *home!*

Having arrived from the balmy beaches of Clearwater, Florida. New York's East Village was a mix of shock and relief to the Harris family, shown here in the courtyard of 319 East 9th Street. Photo by Andrew Sherwood, 1965

All eight Harris family members – George Sr., Ann, Walter Michael, Frederic, Jayne Anne, Eloise, Mary Lou and G3 himself – got busy auditioning for plays and commercials, taking voice and dance lessons, obtaining agents, going to photo shoots, needing early wake-up calls, cueing each other on their lines in every available corner of the apartment and of course going to school, doing homework and working the occasional survival job required for rent and groceries. The Harris family was soon dubbed "The Lunts of off-off-Broadway" by Caffe Cino playwright Robert Patrick, a leading light in the fast-growing experimental theater community. The family performed in plays, Be-Ins, happenings, festivals, films and on television during the off-off-Broadway explosion that was the starting line for hundreds of artists who, like the Harrises, were just beginning their careers.

Robert Heide, playwright, on the right, with partner **John Gilman**, left

The East Village was teeming with emerging youthful inspired social energy that fertilized the off-off Broadway theater movement. Civil rights protests, blossoming hippie cultures and human eco-systems of dark poverty lined the dirty city streets with drunks and disenfranchised citizens left over from the stock market crash and the McCarthy Era. The dark and dismal 1960s backdrop of New York City was experiencing an exploding creative Bohemia. The transition from the Beat Generation, which consisted of writers and poets, had influenced the next generation. These powerful creative souls moved towards a theatrical expression resulting in an explosion of eminent writers, artists and café/theater owners who created venues for these works to be seen.

The East Village was also a very *scary* place. Bums, drug addicts and runaways co-existed with writers, actors, poets and artists. The cultural ecosystem became a mixed bag as long-standing working class citizens clashed with the ever-growing, unstoppable hippies and their ideals of peace and free love. This mash-up sometimes turned violent. One of the Harris girls witnessed a young male hippie being beaten in the street with a pipe by a 1950s greaser-type who thought the young boy had violated his daughter.

The Harris family was living in close quarters, making their one-bedroom tenement apartment work for a family of two adults and six children. It soon became apparent that the apartment was too small, so ever-industrious George Sr. built sleeping lofts on the tall walls in to give each kid a "room" and simultaneously free up floor space for the furniture, clothing, piano, drums, guitars, phonograph, work bench, make-up mirrors, a sewing machine and Suki the Siamese cat.

This "six-in-one" headshot from 1968 helped the Harris children find work in a variety of art forms in New York City. The photo of Walter in HAIR by is Dagmar and the other five are by Andrew Sherwood.

The Harris kids' mini-lofts notwithstanding, this close living proximity oscillated between a grand urban camping adventure and an emotional pressure cooker as the boys entered their teens. Hormones were raging and privacy was non-existent. The pressure sometimes led to explosive confrontations between G3 and his father, who pushed each other's buttons as the rest of the family scrambled to stay clear.

Face to Face

with a writer-producer-director-actor

[column of small, largely illegible newspaper text]

"I've played an extra in a milk-shake commercial, been a dead-man in a tv series, posed in sweaters for a mail order catalogue," says seventeen-year-old George Harris III of New York City, noting a few of the bread-and-butter jobs he has held. He has also written, directed and acted in five experimental plays, produced them off-Broadway.

His daily schedule is that of a show-business regular who is only incidentally a high school senior. "I begin the day by dancing to rock and roll. When I don't do it, I feel tense all day. Then I go through voice exercises and practice my audition songs. The current ones are Tonight and Sixteen Going on Seventeen.

"Then I phone my manager to find out if there are readings for me to go to. If not, I zip through my homework, spend an hour and a half at Quintano's School for Young Professionals. Afternoons I make the rounds of casting directors. They have to see you once a month to remember you're alive."

On many days George also has to fit all this around acting and modeling jobs; when one of his own productions is in progress, he has rehearsals in the late afternoon, performs at night. On Saturdays he runs a workshop for would-be actors, six to sixteen.

Their Madness, a spoof of Method acting. His productions earned good notices from the critics.

George's life demands faithfulness to the point of ruthlessness. "When the phone rings in our apartment at three in the morning and a voice asks, 'Can you be on the set at seven?' of course I say yes. If the voice asks, 'Do you have a blue suit?' whether I do or not, I say I do. Then I go out and borrow one."

Although George earns money in big chunks—$25 an hour for modeling, $100 plus residuals for a walk-on in a tv commercial, $250 for five lines in a soap opera—his expenses are also high. He gives fifteen percent of earnings to his manager, pays ten percent to his agent, buys clothes and pays tuition for new photos, acting, singing—no mean feat for

George heard acting during school days in Florida. He read scenes and soon was playing in Shakespeare at a local arts center, parts for children, while five able, his five brothers and sisters began acting too; their mother and father at this time in insurance in New York. At this the family quickly landed in series. The father in New York. Everyone in the family joined modeling and George who to...

In George's absence his brother...

Young Thespian Stars In Stevenson Drama

George Harris Jr., son of Mr. and Mrs. George Harris, 935 El Dorado Ave., Clearwater Beach will open tomorrow at the Paper Mill Playhouse in Millburn, N.J. as Jim Hawkins in "Treasure Island."

Other performances are scheduled at Bucks County Playhouse, Pennsylvania, Tappan Zee Playhouse in Nyack, N.Y., Mineola Playhouse in Long Island, N.Y. and a playhouse in Westport, Conn.

The younger Harris is director of the El Dorado players who produced and acted in a film "The Unsinkable Titanic" last summer and produced the play "Cleopatra, Queen of the Nile" early this spring.

George also appeared this summer as Michael in the television series "East Side, West Side" produced by George Scott in New York City.

GEORGE HARRIS JR.
...plays 'Jim Hawkins'

Engaging the press came easily to G3

Early on in New York, G3 landed a role as Jim Hawkins in the summer stock tour of Robert Louis Stevenson's *Treasure Island* at the famous Paper Mill Playhouse. He soon achieved the goal of every actor when cast in the Broadway play, *The Porcelain Year*, starring Barbara Bel Geddes. The show suffered a quick death in previews and never opened on the Great White Way. But, while this felt like a terrible setback at the time, George never dwelled for long on the closing of a show. He now had a Broadway credit and membership in the actors' union. He was a bona fide professional, barely two years after arriving.

George's parents were cast in a many productions as well. As an actor and director, George, Sr. was a regular in the experimental off-off Broadway movement and was branching out by auditioning for films, television, Broadway, street theater and "bus and truck" tours. Ann accepted as many opportunities as she could squeeze in, while taking care of the six very active children. As their kids grew and became more self-sufficient, George Sr. and Ann found they could take roles in the same shows for weeks at a time, such as jointly appearing in the premiere of Lanford Wilson's *The Rimers of Eldritch* at La MaMa, directed by the playwright, and in summer stock.

G3's parents' approach to life and the arts were very different. His father was methodical, practical and tenacious. He would agonize over character analysis, learning his lines and understanding a play or role in its entirety. Ann's approach was whimsical, intuitive and full of magic, fantasy and wonderment. Both methods were formative for G3. His father gave him roots and his mother gave him wings.

G3 unpacked his theatrical trunk and organized a New York City children's theater troupe, once again calling it The El Dorado Players – the only company for child actors on the off-off-Broadway scene in New York City. George enlisted his brothers and sisters, schoolmates and other teenage thespian acquaintances and *their* brothers and sisters! Ellen Stewart once again gave the Harrises a home – this time, a theatrical home. With her full support the reconstituted El Dorado Players began a successful residency at La MaMa ETC. Ellen called this her "Young Playwrights' Series," an association that gave G3's troupe instant gravitas.

By now G3 had several ideas for theatrical adventures going through his head at the same time. Mere seconds would pass in between show ideas. Theater work and regular schoolwork did not mix well, so Ann enrolled him in Quintano's School for Young Professionals. It was a specialized high school for child actors and models. Fellow showbiz classmates included Nancy Allen (now known for the movie *Dressed to Kill),* Jeff Conway (the television sitcom *Taxi),* and Paul Jabara (Broadway's *HAIR* and the future writer of disco hits *It's Raining Men* and *Last Dance*).

G3's family navigated a steady trajectory upwards in the world of show business. Collectively and individually they were embraced and frequently employed by the pioneering producers, playwrights and directors of the experimental theater scene in downtown Manhattan, as well as by commercial producers "uptown." Both parents and all five of George's siblings were soon performing round the clock at Café La MaMa, Caffe Cino, Judson Poets Theater, The Electric Circus and Theater for the New City, while juggling work, school and life.

Top: Rehearsing an original Harris family musical, There Is Method In Their Madness, *at Café La MaMa in 1966.*
Bottom: L to R: George Harris III, Claudia Tedesco-Colmer, Walter Michael Harris and Elena Mattei.
Photos by James D. Gossage

Claudia Tedesco-Colmer

George's schoolmate, best friend, girlfriend and confidante:

George and Claudia in Central Park, circa 1965

I first met George in Mr. Hoffman's math class at Quintano's School for Young Professionals in November, 1965. Jackie Curtis, Nancy Allen, Pia Zadora, among others, were classmates. He had just finished a run in a Broadway play and had a large publicity photo mounted on cardboard (holding it up). After the boring class, I went over to him and asked about the photo.

He told me in a torrent of words about the show, that he had played the son of the two leads, how kind they were to him. He was wearing a sweater one of the actors had given him. The play had closed after a few weeks. He said he was getting an acting company together and would I be his leading lady. It was quick. We went out to a coffee shop in my neighborhood on the Upper West Side for dinner and he asked me to be his girlfriend. He kissed me on the cheek on that first date. We had in common Bronxville where George's family was from. My grandparents had lived there in the 1930s to the 1960s when they moved back to Manhattan. Our families were Catholic.

We would see each other daily and go on rounds to theatrical agents at George's prompting. I remember one agent had a sign they were not accepting photos/resumes. George, being so optimistic, went in and gave his head shot to the secretary. I can still recall her tearing it up before our eyes and putting it in the trash. Fortunately we were better treated at Café La MaMa where Ellen Stewart called us "the babies" and at Caffe Cino, where Joe Cino would never let us pay.

As George started to branch out and explore the city, he began to meet interesting and flourishing young artists. The scene included painters, dancers, writers, choreographers, actors, lighting and sound designers, film directors and all degrees in between.

George was befriended by amazingly talented, and sometimes tragic and traumatized artists who demonstrated their pain on canvas, stage, and film and in life. They filled the streets, cafes, loft spaces, clubs and theaters in the 1960s. They came from all over the world to be part of the exploding artistic scene in New York City. Being in this new circle of creative beings ignited George's imaginative mind and nourished the seeds of the young hippie flower power man that George Harris III would become.

Cousin Dale Rose, circa mid-1960s

Susan Dale Rose
Writer, equestrian, first cousin

Ruth Colony Harris SoRelle was nobody's idea of a cuddly grandmother. Fierce, independent, bitter, funny, fast-driving and hard-drinking, she insisted that we call her Ruthy rather than Grandma and spoke to us as if we were dimwitted adults rather than children. She fed us steak tartare if she fed us anything at all, and I became a better driver after taking her home in her latest sports car after she had been drinking hard with her equally bitter friends. Grandchildren, apparently, were occasionally useful but brought her no joy.

Nonetheless, in the mid-1960s, she invited the oldest of us cousins – me and Georgie – to spend successive summer weeks with her in her Berkshires cottage. Georgie usually went first, which meant that when my week came I would get to hear of his miscreancy as only our grandmother could recount it.

Grandma Ruthy, iconoclast and early influence

Out of cereal? Georgie ate it all. No milk? Well, he must have drunk all of that as well, and why would you need milk if there was no cereal? Georgie dismantled the tile backsplash she was creating out of salvaged, mismatched tiles and laid them back out again to his own design. Georgie let the banty hens out to seek their freedom. Georgie made jewelry out of the feathers and beads she was saving for a future project. Georgie *brayed show tunes* until she was *near distraction.*

Why did I always suspect that there was an ironic note of admiration in all these complaints about my cousin? And why did I also suspect that I would never quite measure up, lacking his boldness, his charisma, his dash?

I polished the family silver, hearing again the story of how it came to be so dented nearly a century before. I tidied up the family documents, listening intently as Ruthy gossiped about long-dead relatives with an arch cattiness that curled around the room like smoke. I took notes to her direction as she scissored up the news broadcasters to whom she ardently listened and whose grammar and syntax she deplored.

And always Georgie was there in the room with us, laughing up a corner, as something would remind Ruthy of something he had said or done or not done the week before.

Claudia Tedesco-Colmer

In 1966, George met John McKendry, a curator of photographs and prints at the Metropolitan Museum of Art. John was very gracious – he understood that if he took George out, he also had to accept me. John was Canadian and had studied art history in London, so had many English friends. He was friends with Lady Jane Ormsby Gore, daughter of Lord Harlech, the British ambassador to Washington. She was the "Lady Jane" of the Rolling Stones song. I babysat her little one while she and her husband met up with Mick Jagger. After George broke John's heart, John married the very tall and witty Countess Maxine de la Falaise. John escorted us to gallery openings on 57th Street and to French restaurants on the Upper East Side. We would depart from his apartment on West 11th Street each evening to Max's Kansas City, where all the artists and curators hung out. From there George met Henry Geldzahler of the Met and Charles Cowles, gallery owner.

George also met Andy Warhol, who was there nightly at the round table. This led to an unfortunate incident with Warhol. George was still a trusting kid and was invited by Andy to The Factory. George read it wrong, thinking that Andy wanted a date. When he got to The Factory, he was attacked and tortured by some male friends of Andy while Andy watched with pleasure.

They put cigarettes out on him, trying to scare him. He begged them to stop. Finally they let him loose at daybreak. George called me from a payphone, crying and upset. I told him to call the police. He said, "Oh they told me the police won't listen to a faggot." He was too embarrassed and scared. Later in the day we met and he showed me the bruises and [burn] marks on his back. He didn't want his mother to know anything.

We met David Hockney at that time. He drove us around town in a Rolls Royce with Peter, his partner. Later, David and George re-connected in Los Angeles.

In 1966 George met British artist David Hockney, who drew this evocative portrait, perfectly capturing George's new sexy look and attitude. (1)

In 1966, George met "G.D." from Brooklyn, a young city planner in the Mayor's office and sometime writer for the Village Voice. They became a couple, living together and again George had me tagging along for poetry readings at St. Mark's where George met Irving Rosenthal (an editor at Grove Press), Allen Ginsberg and Herbert Huncke. G.D. knew many writers and filmmakers on the Lower East Side. George met Jack Smith through G.D. We three would eat supper at Ratner's or Chinatown. G.D. was always attempting to get George to read the classics or to go back to school. Sometimes George would give the book to me to read and then tell him about it. I recall we did this with *Sons and Lovers* by D.H. Lawrence. G.D. was not fooled. He wanted George to attend Columbia University School of General Studies. He wanted George to be serious and George was very unserious.

When George turned 18, G.D. took us to dinner to an Indian restaurant on 2nd Avenue near his tenement apartment. It was my first taste of Indian food. Later George said to me "I'm getting old; people won't think I'm a beautiful boy." He went on, "I don't want to live past 30." I remembered these words when he died at age 32.

George told me that when he was 13 years old he was raped by a neighbor, a married man who took him to Washington D.C for a long weekend. I don't know if he ever told his siblings.

Robert Heide

I first saw George Harris Jr. in the Jeff Weiss play, *A Funny Walk Home*, which opened at the magical Caffe Cino coffee-house theater on Cornelia Street in Greenwich Village on February 2, 1967. I was then in rehearsal with my new play, *Moon,* which was set to follow the Weiss run on Valentine's Day. The brilliant, riveting *Funny Walk* lead role was performed by Jeff Weiss himself, who played a disturbed psychotic who was just returning from a stay at an insane asylum to his family home in the suburbs of Pennsylvania. Awaiting his arrival on tenterhooks is his mother who was played by Claris Nelson, his father – enacted by Bruce Israel, an uncle who's also a reverend – enacted by Christopher Alport, and his younger brother, a shy, passive teen performed with sensitivity by George Harris Jr. This dynamic living-on-the edge tour-de-force has Jeff playing a character he once said was modeled after himself with such intensity that the walls at the Cino seemed to shake. Seduction, rape, incest, fear and narcissistic rage bordering on murder and mayhem as in a Greek tragedy or Shakespeare's *Hamlet* complete this Oedipal cycle. Weiss let it all hang out and with the actors took the audience by storm in this psychodrama that seemed like reality TV or even a step beyond.

Jeff told me recently that George, Jr., with his thick blonde hair, baby blue eyes and pink cheeks, when playing the part of the young brother done in by the all-encompassing madness surrounding him, somehow managed to shine forth with his innocence intact. The critics agreed that *A Funny Walk Home* was one of the best plays that came out of the 'Theater of the Absurd' movement of the Sixties led by Ionesco, Beckett and Albee. Jeff also told me that he was stunned when George Jr. later in the 1970s emerged in San Francisco as Hibiscus and became the leader of a glittering troupe of actors called The Cockettes, covered with sparkling sequins and fairy dust, performing theatrical musical extravaganzas, jumping up and down dancing and singing 1930s Depression songs.

By mid 1966, young George's artistic and street-savvy immersion was beginning to bear fruit. His sunny attitude, political outlook and sexual orientation were developing at a fast pace. His magnetic attraction for powerful, artistic men could not be confined. At sixteen, the world was his oyster. He was smart, handsome, imaginative, talented and brave.

Chapter 3
"FLOWER POWER"
Allen Ginsberg's Vision

Following President John F. Kennedy's 1963 assassination the civil rights movement in America gathered momentum, blazing its path with Martin Luther King, Jr. leading the way. Cultural and societal barriers were being challenged at every level of society. This assertion was reflected in New York City theater offerings of the late 1960s.

In 1966 George III acted in *The Peace Creeps* at New Dramatists, an anti-war play by John Wolfson, with James Earl Jones, Al Pacino, and Paul Jabara, his former schoolmate from Qunitano's. This play raised George's awareness of the horrors of war and its danger to the nation, to the people of Vietnam and to young people on both sides, at risk of being sent to fight, kill and die. Although the draft was on, a hereditary bone condition spared George and Walter Michael from induction.

It was a transitional time for G3 and his family as they continued to succeed in building their careers. Their off-off-Broadway work led directly to new opportunities as both Georges were cast in Ron Tavel's smash hit satire *Gorilla Queen*, at Judson Poets Theater. In it, father and son played members of a tribe of apes called the *glitz ionas,* and shared a cathartic experience unlike any other, on or off stage.

The New York Times Sunday Arts and Leisure section of March 26, 1967, declared, "In the Parish Hall, the Hippies go Ape."

"'Gorilla Queen' is the freest, wildest, most outrageously mannered theatrical diversion to have hit Off-Off Broadway in many a queer-colored moon. While its content, language, and action may confuse, scandalize or bore, no one will be indifferent to its zany originality, its improbable plot convolutions, or its visual and directorial brilliance."

 - John Gruen, The Pop Scene, *New York Times*, March 26, 1967

*"The audience is perched precariously on folding chairs in the dusty,
rickety choir loft at the Judson Memorial Church in Greenwich Village.
Suddenly an actor* [George Harris Sr.], *dressed in garish, anthropoid
makeup, vaults over the railing and stomps through the startled
spectators onto the stage. Snuffling and grunting like a deranged
chimpanzee, he sticks his tongue out at the audience, grinning,
scratching and chattering in a stream of missing-link 'hooga-moogas.'
Thus begins Ronald Tavel's 'Gorilla Queen,' a hairy, horny spoof of
these muddled times, done as a parody of the Maria Montez jungle
flicks of the 40's."*

- Mel Gussow, *Newsweek*, May 1, 1967

Attracted by the zaniness, audiences flocked to Judson Church to see
Gorilla Queen up in its choir loft theater. After Judson it was picked
up by veteran producer Paul Libin with its cast intact and moved to the
Martinique Theater, opening April 24, 1967 and closing June 18. The
audiences kept coming, the critics kept analyzing (or trying to), and
the two Georges were able to quit their day jobs for the run.

Program cover at Judson Poets Theater

40

Actor David Kerry Heefner recalls in *The Gorilla Was Gay: Remembering Ronald Tavel's "Gorilla Queen"* on OutHistory.org:

"One of the best things to come out of working in *Gorilla Queen* was the friendship that developed between me and George Harris III, who played one of the chorus of Gibbons called Glitz Ionas. George III and his father George II were both in the cast, and were regulars in the Off-Off scene. George III had the space next to me at the makeup table and our conversations led to hikes, movies, lunches and laughter. George, who was a reserved, conservatively dressed seventeen year old at the time, was mature for his age (he had a twenty seven-year-old architect lover), and his parents and siblings, all of whom were involved in theatre, were true 'hippies.'

One night after a performance, while we were still playing on Washington Square South, George III and I started off to get something to eat at a nearby diner. We met a fellow actor on the way, who told us that Joe Cino (cafe-owner and one of the first producers of what would come to be called Off-Off Broadway theatre) while on an LSD trip and bereft at the recent death of his lover, Jon Torrey, had stabbed himself in an attempt to commit suicide. He was in intensive care at St. Vincent's Hospital and needed blood badly. Off we went to St. Vincent's, only to find out that much more blood than was needed had already been donated. Joe Cino didn't survive and died on March 30, 1967, and the Caffe Cino perished less than a year later." (1)

For G3, the triple impact of *The Peace Creeps, Gorilla Queen* and the death of Joe Cino awoke in him a political awareness and a personal metamorphosis. He became increasingly absent from his family's East Village apartment and began to explore the world, traveling between coasts and rooming with friends and lovers. His sexual explorations as a sixteen year-old in the flourishing artistic world of New York City set his course for the journey of a lifetime.

His soul and artistic wanderlust had been activated. His uninhibited free expression and clear vision of peace, love, freedom and happiness was evident and he was getting ready to share it with the world.

Ann and George, Sr. by Andrew Sherwood, East Village, 1967

At this point George Sr. was always working on one show and learning lines for the next, while working several day jobs to pay the rent and keep food on the table. These activities took every spare minute and limited his family time. As G3 began to rebel against boundaries – a natural teenage pattern even without the family's other pressures – tensions would erupt every so often, as George Sr. could not understand where G3 was coming from, and G3 challenged him about many things. Ann sensed her son's transformation and completely understood. She was his most devoted defender and cheerleader and was the first to notice his unique creativity, leadership abilities and charisma. Not knowing where they would lead or where it would take her son, Ann became his biggest champion and most ferocious protector of his self-discovery.

With all the turbulent revolutions around him, and tensions at home, G3 instinctively created an escape. Like Noah, George was about to build a giant ark. Unlike Noah, his would be glittered and feathered and festooned with rhinestones. As if he had put on a pair of magic glasses, he seemed headed toward building a utopian society that he was creating for himself, and anyone who wanted to climb aboard.

Allen Ginsberg's "FLOWER POWER" *manifesto*

The idea of Flower Power as a symbolic action of protest against the Vietnam War originated with poet Allen Ginsberg's 1965 essay titled "Demonstration or Spectacle as Example, As Communication or How to Make a March/Spectacle." In it, Ginsberg advocates that protesters should be provided with "masses of flowers" to hand out to policemen, press, politicians and spectators. The use of props like flowers, toys, flags, candy and music were meant to turn anti-war rallies into a form of street theater, thereby reducing the fear, anger and threat that is inherent within protests. (2)

Walter Michael Harris

By mid-1967, anti-war demonstrations filled the streets and parks of New York City. Political activist Jerry Rubin, with poets Allen Ginsberg and Ed Sanders, led a loose coalition of community organizations called The National Mobilization Committee to End the War in Vietnam. They organized a March on Washington, D.C., scheduled for October 21, with the intention of "levitating" the Pentagon, along with other acts of peaceful resistance.

At Allen Ginsberg's invitation, George accepted a cross-country ride to San Francisco, driven by Allen's partner, Peter Orlovsky. En route, they detoured to the demonstration at our nation's capital. George telephoned me from the road, urging me to get on a bus and participate in the demonstration with him. I elected to pass on his invitation, a decision I would later regret. On October 21 a group of demonstrators, including George, confronted fully armed National Guard soldiers deployed to guard the Pentagon and to keep the demonstrators under control. In that crucible of dangerous tension my brother, eighteen at the time, responded by gently placing flowers in the soldiers' gun barrels.

Ann Harris

When George called me the day after the demonstration he was breathless with excitement and said, "Mom, the press was there and hundreds of photographers taking our picture. I could hear the cameras!"

Walter Michael Harris

This was no surprise, a very George thing to have done. Street theater and living symbolism were concepts he understood and practiced. George wasn't alone, as there were other young people putting flowers in guns as advocated by his friend Allen Ginsberg and his co-organizers of the event.

This historic moment, captured on film by photojournalist Bernie Boston, fixed the idea of Flower Power forever in the public's imagination. It was first runner-up for the Pulitzer Prize that year. Boston's iconic image of George answering guns with flowers remains a metaphor for the hope of the 1960s youth counterculture movement – that love can overcome political tyranny, unite the human family, break the war machine and bring peace to the world.

Courtesy Wendy Fisher, photographer unknown.

Bernie Boston is the photographer of "Flower Power." The image (3) above was struck from the original negative, and given by Boston personally to the Harris family, along with two alternate images. The following excerpt is from "Bernie Boston: View Finder," (4) a 2005 interview with Bernie by Alice Ashe, written for Curio Magazine:

"When I saw the sea of demonstrators, I knew something had to happen. I saw the troops march down into the sea of people," Boston says, "and I was ready for it." One soldier lost his rifle. Another lost his helmet. The rest had their guns pointed out into the crowd, when all of a sudden a young hippie stepped out in front of the action with a bunch of flowers in his left hand. With his right hand he began placing the flowers into the barrels of the soldiers' guns. "He came out of nowhere," says Boston, "and it took me years to find out who he was … his name was Harris."

Inspired by his brother's activism, Walter Michael accepted a role in the rock musical *HAIR,* which gave him the opportunity to demonstrate against the war to a large Broadway audience eight times a week. The show debuted October 17, 1967, at Joseph Papp's New York Shakespeare Festival Public Theater and quickly moved to Broadway, opening April 29, 1968 with new additions to the cast, including Walter Michael Harris.

In 1968 George Sr. was cast in Howard Sackler's Pulitzer and Tony-winning Broadway hit, *The Great White Hope,* co-starring James Earl Jones as a black champion boxer and Jane Alexander as his white girlfriend. Set in the early years of the 20th Century, *The Great White Hope* touched on issues of racism and power in America.

Walter Michael in HAIR, *photo by Dagmar.*

George Harris Sr. (holding newspaper) in The Great White Hope's post-Broadway tour, 1969-1970

PART II
THE COCKETTES

Like a Florida chameleon, George Harris III shed his skin and begin his new adventure with a new name: Hibiscus de la Blossom. Hibiscus created a bejeweled script for his sparkling new free theater. These glittering pages and ornate handwriting represented his transformation into his own Utopia.

Chapter 4
The Summer of Love and
Birth of The Cockettes

"He came out of the closet, wearing the closet."
Nikki Nichols

Hibiscus found freedom, self-expression and other colorful souls when
The Cockettes came together. Here they are playing dress-up in the
attic of the Sutter Street Commune in San Francisco.
Harris family archive photo, circa 1969

The Summer of Love in 1967 attracted an unprecedented gathering of
young hippies to San Francisco. As 1968 dawned, the good will and
optimism of that summer continued to draw all kinds of Flower Power
people to the Haight-Asbury area. Eighteen-year-old George Harris, III
was no exception. He had just performed the ultimate Flower Power
act in Washington, D.C. and was eager to build on the catharsis of that

moment by doing whatever was needed. He started by giving himself a complete makeover, physically and spiritually.

Mark Thompson's profile of, and interview with, **Hibiscus** in his book, *Gay Spirit: Myth and Meaning* –

> According to Allen Ginsberg, the precocious young actor had a circle of friends that included Irving Rosenthal, who had edited William Burroughs's Naked Lunch at Grove Press, and filmmaker Jack Smith, whose *Flaming Creatures* remains a classic of independent cinema. Both men espoused controversial and visionary points of view through their work. "Jack Smith's film involved dressing people up in transsexual costumes with great adornment; veils and spangles and beautiful makeup. And Irving had the theory of having everything free," said Ginsberg. "So Hibiscus brought all that new culture west."
>
> Hibiscus had an offer to drive west with Peter Orlovsky and another friend. **[Hibiscus speaking]:** "I was still very Brooks Brothers – you know, short hair and lots of madras shirts. I was lucky to catch the whole love-child bit just in time."
>
> "I started to grow my hair and became a vegetarian. I lived the life of an angel there. I was celibate and started to wear long hair and headdresses. I'd go down to Union Square and run around singing all my old Broadway show favorites: 'You Are Beautiful,' 'If I Loved You'." (1)

San Francisco's Haight-Ashbury district was the epicenter of the hippie revolution, and a melting pot of music, psychedelic drugs, sexual freedom, creative expression and politics. This new utopian and tolerant society allowed for thousands of closet doors to burst open, and just as many transformed souls would make their entrances with a newfound cornucopia of freedoms, opulence and identities. Young George announced his new identity as Hibiscus de la Blossom, which continued his lifetime themes of free expression and Flower Power.

Hibiscus dancing with a baby on Hippie Hill in 1969, Golden Gate Park, San Francisco, by Robert Altman

Robert Altman, Photographer
A Short Cockette Memoir

During The Sixties I lived in a metropolis sporting straights, longhairs, anti-war activists and parading hippies. Marvelous mayhem amid the tumult and the turbid. I thought I had seen everything. I mean, hadn't we gone as far as we could go?

No.

No, no, no, no, NO!

Enter..."The Cockettes!" What a jaw dropper that first sighting was. I was on assignment and spent 4 days living with them in their communal household; sweated dress rehearsals and finally gussied up for their opulent opening night at The Palace Theatre.

It seemed that a new, inflamed and colorful species metamorphosed. They knew they were torrid and they knew there was nothing else on earth like them. Their magnetism was white hot and I basked in their glow while recording some of the most colorful images ever.

I must admit that I was most touched, indeed drawn to Hibiscus, their guiding light and founder. There was that certain 'something' about him. Gentle, graceful, winsome, fey. I could add a hundred more positive adjectives that would never capture this sprite's nature. I'll say this though...I am straight...but if ever there was someone who I'd let take me through that lavender garden it would have been Hibiscus.

James Windsor, aka Tahara
West Coast Angel of Light

Irving Rosenthal, a writer, artist and highly intelligent, rather idealistic character, began telling young people he met about his vision of communal living and eventually a few interested young types came to live with him. At first, they were all taking psychedelic drugs, smoking marijuana and exploring their consciousness. At some point Irving, as the leader of the house, had taken an interest in a local hippy group called The Diggers. They were a revolutionary minded group, based on an idealistic 17th century group of the same name in England. The San Francisco group had also adopted the same philosophy and interesting work ethic as the original Diggers in that they believed that heaven could be created on earth through selfless service.

From the Diggers, Irving formulated ideas on how his commune should function as a free selfless-service community group. Irving also decided the commune would maintain a constructive work environment by having daily work projects in which members would participate with each other, thereby forming relationships based not only on friendship but also on working together.

Among the communal work projects started was the publication of a weekly communal newsletter called *Kaliflower*. The name was taken from the goddess Kali and the word "flower" added for flower power. It was a free newsletter whose purpose was to encourage others to live communally and to do selfless service.

Because of Hibiscus' lack of interest in communal rituals, Irving eventually asked him to leave the commune. Fortunately, while living at Irving's, Hibiscus had acquired government assistance, keeping him safe from hunger and giving him the ability to pay rent elsewhere.

He began to meet other unusual artists outside of the commune who were interested in theater – and with this new group of friends, Hibiscus decided to form an actual theater group, called The Cockettes. Hibiscus began a new life of theater, art, drag, psychedelics, glitter and homosexuality.

Society played its part as the ideal stage in which to shine his brightest beacon of light in order to attract other like-minded people who otherwise would have been forced to dim their souls in any other era. One by one, Hibiscus found his tribe and intoxicated them with his flair – much like animals do when they shake their hindquarters or fully open their gills and tails in a ritual of mating and attraction.

Hibiscus, San Francisco, circa 1970

Hibiscus – A letter to his brother Walter Michael, early 1969:

Some other spring
Now I still cling
To faded blossoms
Thus sings Billie Holiday.

Dear Walter,

A bizarre morning here in San Francisco. The wind howls as I howl. I remember last night running through China Town with flowers and glittering red Chinese banners flapping in the wind. Running from the horrors. I seek pure light, I seek the Kingdom of God. Life is so fleeting and I find myself leaving the path, then discover myself surrounded by darkness.

O to be crystalline - I have been living in a world of twilight... I lay on the scaffold like Christ on the cross. Sunshine, the stars, the moon, my view of Toledo, the glittering lights of Uranus and the hills of San Francisco. A mosque from my window.

So many new faces here at the commune. Rain pouring down at all the windows, I'm thinking of New York City. Wishing I could be there with you tonight. Sometimes when I wake up in the morning I think that you are still here on Sutter Street. So strange to be living up in the clouds.

I live with the angels of light. You have nothing to fear from the earthquake. And if death should come we shall all hold hands and descend into spirits. Come here and purify your soul. I hope for Fred to come here this summer, tell him a loft will be built in the sky.

Today is Tuesday. I find myself a kitchen slut crying at the fire by a burning rose. I collect orange peels and faded blossoms, O golden roses, a lost hand to make up for lost love. I have given up forks and chopsticks and eat with my fingers like some forest creature. Let all the animal in yourself flow, make no mistake. Look to the stars.

I shall fast and not break these vows of silence to find once more the grace of God and prayer. Feeling released from the shackles of Karma, waiting to hear love's magic music.

I speak to you through a veil of tears.
Love, Hibiscus

Walter Michael: He closed with this postscript:

*"The waitress held the rose and sniffed it ten times over, her
life of longing had been fulfilled. I love to watch people on the
streets to become them, to change their lives. All the children
of Paradise."*

*Hibiscus' identity as a gender-bending, gay-spirited, mythological
creature was a perfect metaphor for pure freedom of self-expression.
Photo: Harris family archives.*

Jilala, aka Jim Jet, James Tressler
Hibiscus' friend from the Kaliflower Commune

Once upon a time when the homeland was at war, senselessly,
with an irrelevant enemy – actual enemy China – a surrogate
war – and the whole nation shuddered, its brightest youth,
poets and actors fled traditional turf for this backwater
Baghdad 1967 – and figuring I had signed up for a strict

priesthood I was enormously thrilled that this gadfly to Irving existed and if he hadn't I would've. I remember one night most of all when I was awakened by George kissing my neck begging me to intervene with Irving who had asked him to leave. I never felt that way with Hibiscus, as he was more than a love object, he had a visible following like the Aurora Borealis or meteor showers.

Of course the shows he would manage to produce had as a cast his devotees – and oddly enough each show in the early days would incorporate a wedding into the script with Hibiscus's latest love as the groom du jour. Jesus proved himself to his throng with bread and fish, George came through every time with an infectious hilarity, a zaniness one might see as a skin he wore, a fleshy coat to mesmerize the stage door johnnies.

He was not messianic. He was a mess. The art of drawing a show into existence is the absolute proof of his power. Sequins and glue-guns and yards of lamé fell into his lap. The chaos of backstage with him is more the secret than onstage. He would pace, a severe look like Richard Burton about to do his Hamlet. And no less an actor was our beloved George.

At home when things weren't going his way he would hide under blankets saying he had the "vapors." Some Ante-bellum femme fatale to be sure – his fan was fluttering a lot. When attaching the black wings for the Halloween show they kept falling off. He said, "Staple them to my head!" Leonce had just given him his B12 shot.

In that self same Civil War dress he wore, he and I went into Old St. Mary's singing MINE EYES HAVE SEEN THE GLORY...we were thrown out by the priests forthwith. He and I wore double blond wigs and mucho lipstick and both thrown out of the Stud forthwith. He as the Virgin Mary and whole (it was Xmas Eve) troupe was scattered by the police at Grace Cathedral. So much for icons.

56

Jilala (in hat with fan), Jeri, Tahara and Tulah in San Francisco, early 1970s. Courtesy James Tressler.

His next show was *Lola-Lola, Lola-Lola and Lola Lola* – the three Lola's – I was number three. A rare stage adventure for such a nerd as I. He would say "are you excited?" again and again. Much will be said of him but I remember most the thrill of finding rags in abandoned buildings with Rosalind and Ira Cohen and him hopping through the desolation to come up with some Deco drape or tattered blouse.

Like an advance team from Outer Space we walked through the crumbling Western Addition neighborhood decimated by a vast gentrification. I shall always remember him walking sorrowfully back to the encampment we had set up on a commune trip to Death Valley. He had set out alone, naked, only to have fallen and returned all bloodied, his cock too.

My favorite show with him was at the Longshoreman's Hall in SF. He got me to play Mammy in blackface and sing FISH GOTTA FLY with him – he plied me with whiskey. He ripped rare photos out of library books of Nijinsky plastering them around his bed to remind us and himself who he really was at heart, this erotic sprite with a hyena laugh whom I shall miss all the days left me by God my Ziegfeld.

Adrian Milton – Cockette and Angel of Light
Photo: Adrian from the show Peking on Acid.

I first met Hibiscus in 1968. I was sitting in the Panhandle with a few friends and I noticed a person flitting in and out of the bushes. He was all dressed in white with rouged cheeks and flowers in his hair. He came towards us and handed me a note (which I still have). The note was written on a brown paper bag. Hibiscus was silent, not speaking at the time, in emulation of the guru Meher Baba. At that time he was going by the name Baptiste, a character in the French film that depicted a theater company named the Angels of Light. The note read: "Tender Shepherd, Tender Shepherd, Help me lead My Sheep. Bombay Baby, Bombay Baby." I smiled, he bowed and then flitted away.

Shortly thereafter he had the idea for The Cockettes. Hibiscus was living at Kailiflower and I went to visit him about a week later. We had dinner. I didn't like the vibes at Kaliflower. Much too controlling and rigid for my taste. After dinner Hibiscus and I made love. Sex was more of a sorting out process between us than an erotic event.

One of the great things about Hibiscus is that he was not restrained by a formal education. As a result he would mix and match characters to his personal fantasy and create very original scenarios. His sense of costume was superb and unequaled in the Bay Area. One would often see him wafting through the neighborhood and it was like an apparition from a Mystery Play.

One afternoon Hibiscus, myself, and Raggedy Robin, dressed in our splendid best, went up to a Carmelite convent for the Consecration of the Eucharist. The nuns were cloistered behind a screen. They had taken a vow of silence but they were singing while the priest conducted the ceremony. We were the only people in the congregation and the nuns were peering sideways at us. I am sure that they were unsure as to what they were seeing.

I went to India and spent almost a year there. When I returned to San Francisco, Scrumbly invited me to join The Cockettes.

Every year the Krishna people would hold a festival in San Francisco to honor Krishna, called the Great Rathayatra. An image of Krishna was atop a great juggernaut float. Everyone was assembled on Haight Street waiting for the march to begin. I was dressed as Krishna, my face painted blue and adorned in Indian costume. I had a single peacock feather protruding from a band around my forehead. This upset the Krishna people because apparently no one but Krishna may wear the feather in this manner. Hibiscus had a spectacular headdress of white ostrich plumes and was wearing an Afghan shawl.

It was very hot and everyone was waiting for the procession to start. I asked my cousin, Beau, what we were waiting for. He replied, "They are waiting for you to start." So I stepped out on to Haight Street with Hibiscus and my cousin Beau and we proceeded ahead. At that point everyone followed. Everyone was chanting and dancing and we were all in a state of near-ecstasy. Of course helped along by copious amounts of pot.

After a wonderful march through the park we arrived at the beach. There were a few campfires and we sat down by the fire facing the ocean. Allen Ginsberg came over and joined us, followed by Joni Mitchell, who began to sing. As the sun set over the Pacific, we all slowly made our way back to The Haight. I remember this day vividly and cherish the thought of it.

Adrian Milton and Hibiscus at the Great Rahayatra Festival, Golden Gate Park, San Francisco, 1969

Continuation of Mark Thompson's profile of, and interview with, Hibiscus in his book, *Gay Spirit: Myth and Meaning* –

Mark Thompson: The city was alive with counterculture entertainment. The Grateful Dead and the Jefferson Airplane gave regular concerts in the parks, and groups like The Committee and the Floating Light Opera attracted large followings. A small movie theater in North Beach, The Palace, was also featuring Nocturnal Dream Shows at midnight. "I wanted to do a New Year's show," Hibiscus recalls, "and the Palace invited me to do it there.

Hibiscus: About eight of us – including Dusty Dawn, Scrumbly, Goldie Glitters and Kreemah Ritz – got up on stage in drag and danced to an old recording of 'Honky Tonk Woman.' The audience surged toward the stage, screaming. I was dumbfounded."

60

Hibiscus with Divine,
circa 1970

Mark Thompson: As the psychedelic San Francisco of the '60's began evolving into the gay San Francisco of the '70's, The Cockettes, a flamboyant ensemble of hippies (women, gay men, and babies) decked themselves out in gender-bending drag and tons of glitter for a series of legendary midnight musicals at the Palace Theater in North Beach. With titles like *Tinsel Tarts in a Hot Coma* and Pe*arls over Shanghai*, these all singing, all dancing extravaganzas featured elaborate costumes, rebellious sexuality, and exuberant chaos.

The 1970s had begun; The Cockettes were born. The Cockettes created a whole series of shows. The first few years were rough as the group got more and more popular and "everybody" became a friend of The Cockettes. Some of their "friends" included: Janis Joplin, the Grateful Dead, Jefferson Airplane and John Lennon. (1)

The Cockettes struck a powerful chord in the chaos of the hippie Mecca. Their joy, freedom of spirit and unending energy to entertain suddenly became a celebration for the citizens who built and lived their utopian dream of living in peace, freedom, love, happiness, and Flower Power.

The Nocturnal Dream Shows, Kaliflower and the Birth of The Cockettes

By Martin Worman (right) with Robert Croonquist (left)

From *Midnight Masquerade*, unpublished dissertation of Martin Worman, 1992

The Cockettes were an unannounced act between films at the Nocturnal Dream Show's New Year's Eve party. Two San Francisco Art Institute film students, Steven Arnold and Michael Weise, began producing the Nocturnal Dream Shows early in 1969, presenting rarely-seen classic cinema and new underground films at the Palace Theater in North Beach on Fridays and Saturdays at midnight . . . Originally intended as an opera house, the Palace was designed in a streamlined Chinese deco style. Although there had been remodeling in the 1950s, the theater remained elegant in its details, which included rattan chairs in the lobby, recessed water fountains in chartreuse and red tiles, and swirling comets on the Oriental carpeting. The growing popularity of the Nocturnal Dream Shows encouraged an independent producer named Sebastian to take more chances in programming, "At midnight, people would come for whatever was being shown in hopes of getting blown away and there was so much they hadn't seen before." One midnight-to-dawn extravaganza for an early Fall weekend, for example, included *Duel in the Sun*, *Flamingo Road* and *A Dream of Wild Horses*, shown with Maria Montez and Jean-Pierre Aumont in *Siren of Atlantis*, George Kuchar's *Color Me Shameless*, the weekly installment of a *Flash Gordon* serial, plus a clip of Hedy Lamar's nude scene from

62

Ecstasy. The following week, *Me and My Brother* with Allen Ginsberg and Peter and Julius Orlovsky had its San Francisco premiere at the Palace on a double bill with Todd Browning's *Freaks*. And the week after that, Sebastian programmed the local debut of Jack Smith's *Flaming Creatures* shown along with the expressionist classic *The Golem*. According to John Rothermel, Smith's film provoked an epiphany. Many of the people who eventually became Cockettes were profoundly moved by the film and when they arrived in New York almost two years later the influence was noted by the local cognoscenti.

For Halloween 1969, Sebastian wanted to do something special. Although every Nocturnal Dream Show looked like Halloween, he persuaded The Palace's owner Mr. Chew to cancel the evening showing of the scheduled Chinese film, so that the party could start at 9 p.m. . . "Many surprises! Come in costume!" the poster urged, "All tickets $3.00!"

Among the spectator-participants on Halloween was Hibiscus, a member of the Kaliflower commune on Sutter Street. He arrived at the Palace wearing a shocking pink Jayne Mansfield gown with beach ball breasts, Kabuki make-up and glitter in his beard, topped by a floor-length bridal veil trailing 15-feet behind him and carrying arms-full of dead roses. Steven Arnold recalled that "when he entered the theater, I just bowed. We would never dream of charging him. I said 'You ought to do something on the stage,' and he said, 'I'd love to.'" That night Sebastian remembered first seeing Hibiscus earlier in the year at Land's End, the gay cruising beach, "Of course at Land's End everyone was mostly naked, Even so, Hibiscus always managed to drape something natural and decorative over himself."

The Evolution of Hibiscus and the Kaliflower Commune

The audience that fell in love with the Cockettes at the Nocturnal Dream Shows was composed of a growing mélange of regulars: pot-smoking/acid-head film buffs, older beatniks, younger hippies, artists, intellectuals and adventurous swingers from all parts of the city as well as politicized and thrill-seeking collegians from Berkeley, Stanford and other Bay Area schools. They all came to partake of and contribute to the late-night gambolings of San Francisco's underground,

George Harris III evolving into Hibiscus de la Blossom, flower child and founder of The Cockettes. Photos by (clockwise from left) Andrew Sherwood, Walter Michael Harris and Ingeborg Gerdes

fostered by the deco ambience of the Palace Theater in its historically bohemian North Beach location. It was from that very audience that the Cockettes emerged. Besides John Rothermel, Frank Bourquin, Goldie Glitters and Hibiscus, other future Cockettes had already been spectators at the Palace. Some of them met there for the first time, but by and large they had all previously met Hibiscus elsewhere in town.

A twenty-one year-old transplanted New Yorker who'd been living in San Francisco for two years, Hibiscus organized the group for the 1969 New Year's Eve show . . .

In 1967, it was Irving Rosenthal and Peter Orlovsky who brought the then eighteen-year-old George Harris III (two years before he changed his name) on a cross-country drive from New York to San Francisco. Peter Orlovsky had just acquired a new cream white Volkswagen van and offered to drive Rosenthal and a small entourage, including George.

The van arrived in San Francisco in the fall of 1967, but it wasn't until nearly two years later that George lived with Irving. While Rosenthal sought to establish his commune, George moved into a flat with friends of Rosenthal's on Hayes Street. George made at least one extended trip back to New York during the two years, but he always kept in touch with Irving and continued to express interest in his commune and "free" philosophy. "Free" was a Utopian lifestyle, which didn't include money. It was based on barter and exchange of services and giving freely even if people couldn't "pay" in some way. Rosenthal envisioned a society where nothing would be paid-for with earned money but exchanged with labor based on the value of the goods and services received, including art and entertainment. He felt that art, especially, must remain outside of the money cycle. When living communally, all the bills that needed to be paid to the unenlightened sector still dealing with money (landlords, for example), would be met by the welfare checks and trust funds (free money) of the communards.

Rosenthal established the Kaliflower commune in 1969 when he acquired two flats in a Victorian house on Sutter Street in lower Pacific Heights. He was finally able to put his ideas into practice. Kaliflower became one of the organizers of an inter-communal food-buying cooperative that pooled labor and food stamps to provide low cost, quality food from Bay Area farmers markets to collective households in town. Although each household shared in the process of taking food orders, going shopping, etc., Kaliflower specialized in home-delivering the produce. With Rosenthal at its head, Kaliflower also included writing and publishing as part of its collective mission. The commune wrote, designed and printed *Kaliflower*, a weekly magazine of practical, philosophical and political household tips, which they delivered with the groceries.

Before allowing George to join Kaliflower, however, Irving tested him with a month-long trial period as a day worker. Apparently Rosenthal still looked upon the young man as an ambitious actor-model with no real alternative consciousness; but George seems to have passed the test with many flying colors. Rosenthal's disdain turned into the bemused admiration of a no-nonsense schoolmarm with a soft spot:

"He had a keen sense of beauty and was a generally good influence. He helped cook, later drew for *Kaliflower*, and slowly metamorphosed from a young uptown faggot to the airy spirit that later dubbed himself Hibiscus. He started wearing turbans, then sticking a few fern leaves in them, then more, until, over a period of months, his headdresses turned into tropical islands of vegetation. He went barefoot and started wearing full rag drag full-time: torn gowns, flowing coat linings and tattered scarves . . . His room became a jungle of drag, items of personal adornment, dried flowers, photos make-up, illustrations cut out of library books, love letters, incense and vaseline."

Left: Ralif, photo courtesy Robert Croonquist, right: Hibiscus exploring his identity, circa 1969

Ralph Sauer, aka Ralif, a fellow communard at Kaliflower, claimed that Irving Rosenthal was the sole ruler of his house, and it was Irving who pushed Hibiscus into his new being, "Irving always said 'More! More pampas grass! More robes!' It was Irving who prodded everyone into being more than they were." Sauer also believed that Rosenthal was a "truthsayer who would say things you didn't want to admit to yourself. He had a keen eye for people's faults and weak spots, and he'd point things out to you which your pride rejected." Most of the time Ralif felt that Irving's observations were unsolicited and uncalled-for and claimed that other people variously considered him a rabbi-therapist, a visionary utopian and a sexual fascist. Rosenthal, however confessed to Ralph that, "simply, I love to meddle." Sauer further stated that "Irving would give directives, like taking off your clothes when someone's parents visited. And he pressed for sexual liberties." Sauer followed the orders, believing that at Kaliflower he had "met the Pantheon, and was living amongst the gods."

Hibiscus's life of service at Kaliflower had its highs and lows. Ralph Sauer recalled, "Hibiscus and I would spend hours dressing just to come down to cook dinner! We would sing at the top of our lungs. The fiery gypsy wenches! The kitchen sluts!" One of Hibiscus' favorite things to do in the kitchen was to scramble up on the table while Ralph was cooking and fart in his face. At other times on kitchen duty, Hibiscus would hide in the pantry violently banging his head against the wall because of something Irving had said. Sauer explained that, "Irving's criticism could be on any issue, anything minor like about a trick the night before, or a piece of bread with honey left on the table, an oversight." Between license and discipline, Hibiscus discovered his own true name while reading Jean Genet's *Our Lady of the Flowers*. He wrote of this and other events in letters to his family in New York. Brother Walter Harris was in the New York tribe of *Hair* on Broadway in April 1969, when he received a letter, which reveals some of the newly blossomed Hibiscus' vision: "I find myself a kitchen slut crying by the fire by a burning rose. I collect orange peels, faded blossoms . . . I love to watch people that I see on the streets, to become them, to change their lives. All the children of Paradise."

The Kitchen Sluts

It was as an act of service that the Kitchen Sluts took their at-home antics to other people's houses. Believing that all hippies were straight except for those at Kaliflower, Hibiscus hit upon a plan to reach out to other gay blossoms he was meeting through the food co-op. "One day I was scrubbing the kitchen floor with Ralph and I said why don't we do shows? We'll call ourselves 'The Kitchen Sluts' and go from commune to commune with our deliveries, singing and dancing."

"There were three kitchen sluts," Ralph Sauer recalled, "Jilala, Hibiscus and myself. We got the name from Aldonza's song in *Man of La Mancha*, 'Won't you look at me, look at me, God won't you look at me? Look at the kitchen slut wreaking of sweat!'" Hibiscus, Ralph and Jilala's musical comedy-inspired carryings-on while delivering the groceries, made instant audiences of people in their own homes; and along the way, the Kitchen Sluts found a core of kindred souls ready to act-out their own theatrical fantasies as well.

Cockette Kreemah Ritz remembered Hibiscus' food deliveries, which began in late Spring 1969, "He was always very flirtatious and highly dressed up. I never saw him without rings in his nose, feathers in his headdress, the flowers and grass skirts, bare feet and black toenails. We instantly had a lot in common. We always talked about theater and concerts and old movies, whatever was playing in town. We started talking about doing a show sometime, somewhere. It wouldn't be for money, but just something to put on for friends." Although a participant in the food co-op, Kreemah had no knowledge of the Nocturnal Dream Shows until many months later when Hibiscus invited him for dinner at Kaliflower on New Year's Eve.

December 31, 1969

And so it was through communal, artistic and sexual affinities that various people were introduced to Hibiscus, to each other, and to the midnight events at the Palace Theater. Most of them knew less than a week beforehand about the New Year's Eve appearance; and although some of each of them had met during the course of 1969, they didn't

<u>all</u> meet until that last night of the year. In an interview given in the early 1980s, Hibiscus remembered:

Screen shot from Luminous Procuress, *1970. Kreemah Ritz, Hibiscus*

"New Year's Eve, Irving and all the big 'free' people were going to be away. I decided we should do a show, and I called all these people I had met like Goldie Glitters and Kreemah Ritz, from stops on my food delivery route. They said 'Yes'...We were going to go out and do a show in the street, until I remembered the Nocturnal Dream Shows. I called up Steven Arnold, and he said 'Sure!'"

Sebastian offered another version of the New Year's Eve arrangement. He revealed that he and Link Martin had met at the Palace in the Spring of 1969 and had an affair that lasted most of the rest of the year. During the Summer, Link moved across the Bay to Berkeley where his innately radical inclinations were further politicized. The police storming of People's Park, which was reborn in flames as Ho Chi Minh Park, moved him toward Maoist cultural revolution. Also, having been homosexually active since he was a child, Link was transported by news of the Stonewall Riots in New York. Although Sebastian and Link's affair cooled down by late Autumn, they remained friends. Link

69

moved back to the flat on Bush and Baker, and he and Scrumbly Koldewyn pushed the idea of doing a show with Hibiscus and the others. It was Link who officially asked Sebastian if he and his friends could perform at the Palace. While Hibiscus received the initial invitation to perform onstage from Steven Arnold months before, Sebastian claimed it was Link who arranged the New Year's Eve appearance on short notice.

Steven Arnold and Michael Wiese planned a "Futurama Costume Gala" to welcome in the 1970s on December 31, 1969. Sebastian booked a sci-fi program featuring Buster Crabbe as Flash Gordon in *The Purple Death*, (complete, not just an episode), George Pal's *When Worlds Collide* and H.G. Wells, *Things to Come*. "And on stage," the poster titillated, "Golden Toad Magic! Come in Costume and Stay all Night!" The event made John Gleason's

Marquee of The Palace Theater, North Beach, San Francisco

entertainment column in the *San Francisco Chronicle* as a "best bet" for New Year's Eve. The Cockettes were not named in the New Year's Eve publicity. Indeed, they were not a group and didn't have a name, but Hibiscus spread the word early in the week to some of those people he had met over the previous months through the food co-op deliveries or at the Palace or on the strand at Land's End. He made calls and invited them to dinner at Kaliflower. On the afternoon of the performance, the three Kitchen Sluts were plotting around the stove and trying to think of a name while preparing the meal for the expected guests. Hibiscus said, "It should sound something like the Rockettes." And Ralph immediately replied, "The Cockettes!"

70

Promo postcard for The Cockettes, *the acclaimed 2002 documentary co-directed by David Weissman and Bill Weber. Photo by Bud Lee*

About a dozen people arrived at Kaliflower that evening. At dinner Hibiscus announced that "We've got an engagement at the Palace Theater, we go on sometime around 1 a.m." He also announced that he was bringing a 45 rpm single of "Honky Tonk Woman," and that would be their dance music. Nothing else was planned. After dinner everyone was invited upstairs to get ready, using whatever was available. Ralph hadn't approved of Hibiscus taking his act to the Palace because money would be charged at the box office, but he did abet the event by his own act of rebellion against Irving. Irving was out-of-town, but Ralph had access to the drag room in the attic where Irving jealously kept the costumes for a film he was making. Ralph agreed to unlock the door, and turn his back.

The room contained racks of dresses, lingerie and cartons of fabric and other items hoarded from thrift shops and free boxes. An adjoining room had walls of mirrors surrounded by Christmas tree lights; and tables cluttered with wigs, make-up and accessories. Irving had colorful stuffed satin palm trees and monkeys made as decor for his film, and some of them were carried to the Palace to be used as props.

Four of the beautiful Cockettes, clockwise: Sweet Pam aka Pam Tent;
James Windsor, aka Tahara; John Rothermel, and Scrumbly Koldewyn.
Photo of Sweet Pam by Clay Geerdes; others, Harris family archives

Kreemah was able to accommodate a number of people in his vintage Cadillac Fleetwood limousine, while others went down by bus or thumb. The entourage included more than the people who performed. There were roommates, lovers and children, or as Kreemah preferred, "groupies, dressers and people who held our drugs for us."

The Cockettes followed the Floating Lotus Opera Company unannounced and entered so quickly that some spectators thought they were part of the same set. Hibiscus wore a fringed lampshade on his head, coconut halves for breasts on his bare chest and a grass skirt with nothing underneath. Kreemah sported a platinum marcelled wig done-up with red cock feathers and a red velvet Empire dress and danced tango-style with one of the satin palm trees. Harlow's natural blond hair fell in pre-Raphaelite cascades. She wore emeralds at her ears and neck and a backless silver satin gown cut-low in front with a white fox fur draped over her shoulders that allowed her to discreetly flash her breasts. Dusty Dawn wore pigtails and a sailor blouse and swayed to the music while exposing her breasts. Scrumbly also flashed, lifting his hoopskirt to jump through a hula-hoop.

They danced offstage and waved goodbye to their new fans, as Sebastian announced over the loudspeaker, "Ladies and Gentlemen, the fabulous Cockettes!" Hibiscus was amazed. "We just danced all dressed up in drag—that's all we did. The audience went wild and rushed the stage, just from that one little thing." From the very beginning, the Palace audience created the Cockettes. The audience's wild response to the tacky, unrehearsed antics onstage New Year's Eve prompted the producers to invite the troupe back to do more of the same at a show the following month. At that point, the Cockettes weren't a group. Indeed, they had named themselves as a joke only that afternoon. Yet, spontaneously and without seeming intention, the year of chance meetings with new like-minded acquaintances--from San Francisco's streets and parks, beaches and bars, to the food network and the venue provided by the Nocturnal Dreams Shows—made it possible for Hibiscus and his friends to answer a community's yearning for a wild new theater that would represent and celebrate their lives. (2)

Lendon Sadler

Founding Cockette
Abridged interview from Prairie Pop:
Flashback to '70s SanFran drag with former Cockette:

"One day I was in Golden Gate Park," Sadler recalled, "and there was an area called Hippy Hill, and Hibiscus was in a tree and he was singing 'Madame Butterfly' in that high screechy falsetto he would do — and he was just so seductive."

"Hibiscus was a free spirit and he was all over the place. He would hitchhike in dresses. He had long blonde hair and a beard, and he'd wear makeup when he cared to. I mean, first of all, he freaked all the hippies out. We were obviously hippies, but he cornered another market in freakiness, and he began to amass various circles –people with like minds.

"Everybody was raised by somebody, and all of us carried the baggage of our families — our class, our religion, all of those things. The magic of the Cockettes was that everybody showed up and we all flew into a common religion, the Cockettes," he continued. "All of us felt like we were alien creatures born into the world that we had no understanding of, and we were just getting the confidence to say, 'Whatever we are, we are going to push it in your face and we demand to be ourselves'." (3)

Andrew Blauvelt

Director of the Cranbrook Art Museum in in Bloomfield Hills, Michigan

The Cockettes' self-styled outrageous and inventive costumes – that is, when clothing was worn at all – and exuberant make up featuring

bold colors and glitter-dusted beards, created an utterly unique visage that would capture the imagination of its many followers. Often performing a mix of show tunes and original compositions, the group preferred spontaneous performance to extensive rehearsal. Their late-night shows at the Palace Theater in San Francisco drew large crowds and extensive media coverage, unleashing the specter of the gay psychedelic hippie onto the city's countercultural scene.

With their work-life commune and life-as-art philosophy, the Cockettes lived a powerful social and political reality within an alternative world of sexual liberation. (4)

The Cockettes in Steven Arnold's Luminous Procuress, *1971. Hibiscus is seated, center. Photo by Ingeborg Gerdes*

L to R: Anton (Reggie) Dunnigan and Hibiscus in "Fairytale Extravagana, early 70s. Photo by Fayette Hauser

Chapter 5
The Counter-Culture -
Evolution of The Cockettes

"the Cockettes are sexual outlaws"
The Organ - **San Francisco newspaper**

Fayette Hauser – Founding Cockette

Excerpts from Interview by Maggie Kelly: ODDA magazine, February 2016 issue 10, Tributes. *Photo: Clay Geerdes*

Original Cockette member Fayette Hauser reminisces about the good times had at The Cockettes' old Victorian house in Francisco's Haight Ashbury neighborhood:

Maggie: Fayette, you were one of the founding members of the famous Cockettes theatre group of the 1960s. Did you have any idea of the significance of what you were creating at the time?

Fayette: At the time we were into creating as magical an experience as possible. It was very significant to me as an artist and to us as a group. I had a lot of art theory and art history in my head from university but it all became real to me through psychedelics. I knew we were creating the New. And our instant popularity meant that we were successfully channeling the energy that was on the street in San Francisco, the direction that our own society was moving towards and the innovations that we were experiencing. The fact that it took the larger society so long to grasp these Truths is what was surprising to me. I think that the psychedelic experience is core to this consciousness that I and the Cockettes were exploring. Petty thinking and meaningless boundaries simply vanished in the face of the greater vision that we all had.

What is your favorite memory from your time living with the Cockettes in the rambling Victorian mansion in San Francisco?

My favorite memory is of the Cockette House itself. Our environment was so highly decorated that is was pure joy to live there. We were constantly on the hunt for that magical item or piece of clothing and if it wasn't on our bodies, it was up on the walls. Then, as we did more shows, the props and drag came home to live with us so it was one great big Magical Fantasyland. It was so all-of-a-piece that it's hard to separate the memories from the space we occupied.

Left to right: Tahara and Hibiscus. Photo by Gregory Pickup, 1971

Everyone in the house had created their own singular environment in their room and Hibiscus' room was a beautiful extension of his unique persona. It was lovely to go into his lair and hang with him. Almost at once he presented his idea of having us all go onto the stage. Up until then our creative ideas were very personal, Hibiscus galvanized our creative energy into a group mind. He had come from underground theatre in New York so his ideas were radical theatre mixed with a cosmic consciousness. What could be better than that? We all dove in and within two months of his arrival we were up on the stage. Hibiscus had no boundaries at all, he was like a timeless explorer riding point in the psychic realm so he pushed us all into seeing greater possibilities and ideas. He led, we followed. (1)

HRH Lee Mentley – The Princess of Castro Street

Of all the centuries to be living in, The Castro the 1970s was an extraordinary time to be alive.

Lee Mentley, from a Theater production of 'Always Two Sides To A Pancake' ... starring Lee and Mink Stole

One bright sunny Easter Sunday morning I, The Princess, arose to tons of jolly at The Hula Palace Salon at 590 Castro Street on the corner of 19th. We Gurls, male & female decided to have a holiday campaign breakfast down the street at Andy's Donuts. The "Royal We's" proceeded to adorn ourselves with appropriate Easter drag. Hats, crowns, gowns, table cloths, leather, feathers, heels, boots, and tons of bundled calla lily dyed vibrant red in our bath tub collected from Golden Gate Park, plus baskets of candy with a mountain of eggs colored at last night's traveling orgy brought home from the Midnight Sun. The festive if somewhat greasy eggies were ready to be given to the boys on the street.

So many men, so many eggs…!

As we a-lighted on Castro and began our stroll towards Market I noticed over my shoulder a bright light glint in my eye from atop Castro Street coming from Noe Valley. It seemed to be rising like the sun in the middle of the street. We thought it might be Baby Jesus arisen to visit us poor gurls in The Castro. We could hear church bells singing, so we thought it must be her…!

We wandered into the street to witness this bright light descend into the valley. The closer the brighter the rapturous vision became. Soon we realized it was Jesus, covered in sparkle, gems, flowers, silk, Chinese lanterns, and stuffed lamby-pies, with a shroud of gold lame shimmering in the morning dew flowing over yards of asphalt.

Cars were swerving to miss the apparition, pulling over to witness the arisen glory of peace, joy and salvation float-by the size of a small truck. Applause was breaking out along the walkways; shouts of hallelujah hallowed as the glory of god passed through the throngs of well-wishers and amazed local Catholic home owners who probably thought their rapture time had come. Or at least their god had heard their fervent cries and finally came to evict us Rat Fucking Hippies from their Holy Land.

We were in giddy awe throwing multi-colored glittered eggs and candy offerings as the Holy Light passed us by proceeding to Market Street up Divisadero Street off, I supposed, on its glorious way to Golden Gate Park for Easter Service or coffee at Mary's.

My dear sweet sister Maggie of Rod Stewart fame visiting from Hollywood's Tap Dancing Fools, looked to me and asked who is that Masked God?

That, my dear, is an Angel of Light. That is Hibiscus…

Hibiscus in San Francisco, circa 1970.
Photo by Joshua Freiwald

Rumi Missabu, Founding Cockette
Interviewed by **Michael Varrati**
Reprinted from Peaches Christ's Drag Dossier #2

Michael Varrati preamble: When Hibiscus began to form The Cockettes in the streets of San Francisco, his fellow group member and drag icon Rumi Missabu was there. "We were lovers, roommates, worked together," Rumi tells me, "we had quite a history together, and have quite a history still." An invaluable resource in putting together this article, Rumi shared wonderful photos and stories of Hibiscus that helped give me an idea of the world The Cockettes inhabited, and the sexual maelstrom in which they lived.

MV: Rumi, being rooted in The Cockettes from their inception, you got to see a lot of history unfold from a front row seat. I know The Cockettes essentially began in the streets of San Francisco, but do you remember how you first came together? How did you meet Hibiscus?

Rumi: I sometimes try and remember where we first met, and the only thing I can come up with is on the street. That's kind of how we all met. We would all just see each other on the street in the late 60s, and he would just be saying, "Do you want to be in a show?" He just had that spirit about him that no one else did…he had charisma. The shows sometimes just consisted of us walking down the sidewalk. – laughs – We started our own guerilla street theater, and then eventually brought it to the Palace Theater. We came together like magnets. We came from all different walks of life, but we were drawn together. There were a couple places we all would hang out. There was a bar on upper Grant Street in San Francisco, a gay bar, which had no windows. You couldn't see in, you couldn't see out…that's just how it was back then.

81

Hibiscus and Rumi Missabu in Pearls Over Shanghai
Photo: David Wise, circa 1971

MV: What was your general sense of Hibiscus as a performance artist?

Rumi: He had a very strong off-off-Broadway background. He had performed at La MaMa. Before he met us, he lived in this very strict commune run by a near-cult leader, Irving Rosenthal. Everything in this commune was free, it had to be free. So, rooted in that, Hibiscus held the belief from early on that our performances would be free, and we wouldn't charge for shows. He fought our management tooth and nail to not charge two dollars a head to get into the theater. However, they had to, because there were certain overhead costs involved in putting on a performance.

So, every time we performed, Hibiscus would conspire to liberate the theater. He would throw open the side stage door, and let many people in for free. It was always a bone of contention with management.

MV: When we first started discussing Hibiscus, you sent me pictures of his scrapbook. What can you tell me about that?

Rumi: Hibiscus would steal books from the library, and he'd rip them up...and put the pictures and things in his scrapbook. He'd put glitter and decorate them. He was basically like a shaman, because a lot of the early ideas for our shows were based on the images he created in that book. It would start with a photograph that he'd show to all of us.

MV: Tell me a bit about The Cockettes' migration from the streets to the Palace Theatre. It's my understanding that when you moved to that venue the group began to grow exponentially.

Rumi: Originally, we were a commune of twelve gay men and women, but it was so easy to become a Cockette. All you had to do was show up in drag and jump on stage. From there, you'd be in the next show, and the show after that...there was no wall. People brought their boyfriends, friends, lovers.

83

By two months into our run, when we did our first Halloween show in 1970, Hibiscus and I were on our way out, because there were so many people in the production. It hit a point where Hibiscus lost control. We would do a new show every month, and basically Hibiscus would come up with the idea, and we would run with it. He would say, "Okay, we're doing a fairy tale extravaganza, and I want all the of the fairy tale characters to come together on LSD." And we'd say, "Okay! I'll be the Faerie Godmother, you be this, you be that..." It's just what we did. But, as more and more people came on board, we'd get people who really thought they were in a Broadway show or something, and they would start to take over. It got too serious for us, and it lost something. In fact, they got so serious about it, they created a board of directors within the Cockettes. Hibiscus was so anti-board, it just wasn't him.

Slowly, but surely he became worthless to the new direction the group was taking, and after awhile he'd come to rehearsal and all he was capable of doing was giving blow jobs. He was kicked down the stairs, and booted out. When he begged to come back, they told him no. So, out of solidarity for him, I also quit the group. They went to New York in 1971, and neither Hibiscus nor I went with them. We refused to go. They were bringing two plays we had done into the ground, which were proven successes in San Francisco, to New York. Since we were famous for mounting something new every month, I thought, "Why not create something new?" But, they opened with our old material...and it was a debacle. People fled. It was so hyped up. Also, they had put up posters of Hibiscus there at the theater in New York, despite the fact he wasn't in the show...and his mom went to the theater and ripped them down.

They actually hired a fake Hibiscus for the production, and two fake versions of me! It was a Cockette named Wally, he took on Hibiscus's whole persona. Again, we didn't realize how political we were at the time. We didn't understand the ramifications. We were just out to have a party, and that was Hibiscus's attitude. I always like to say that the content of our shows couldn't have lived in an established world of theater because we were sexual goof-offs. And I believe that. But, it was so celebrated and cutting edge. John Waters said it was like going to a high school reunion at a mental institution. (2)

The Cockettes, photo by Mary Ellen Mark for Paris Match, San Francisco, circa 1970. Hibiscus is top center, in tall feathers.

The 1970s brought sobering realities to Hibiscus and his tribe. Their world was crumbling around them. The hippie message of peace and love, incubated with bountiful amounts of sex and drugs, fueled the potency of a sociological hangover and entertained the beginning of the end of the quest for utopia.

Hibiscus' lightness of being and self-expressing gay spirit was in direct juxtaposition to a Hibiscus-weary committee within the Cockette house. The outlandish societal norms of the Haight-Ashbury allowed Hibiscus to create an environment that encouraged its participants to live in a fantasyland. Despite his demands and stubborn insistence to have the shows (and show business), "his way," he always interacted with the Cockettes tribe as if "only they" mattered. However, Hibiscus was not interested in haters or people changing his vision. It's worth noting here that George's typical compulsive and often bipolar-like behaviors were greatly exacerbated during his time in San Francisco due to his continuous drug-fueled state. This worked

against him in working through disagreements and disputes within the groups.

Conflicting emotions eventually rose to the point of boiling over. His spell had worn off for many of The Cockettes. The natives were restless, angry and hell-bent on overthrowing their leader.

In hindsight, Hibiscus found himself within a fame of sorts, at perhaps too young an age (he was only 22 years old). He had access to freedoms and public praise that went straight to his head. Hibiscus' ego was growing by leaps and bounds. Life became a revolving door of show after show and man after man who wanted to be his lover, cohort or best friend.

Hibiscus in Steven Arnold's Luminous Procuress film, 1971

Lines began to blur between the fire-breathing dragon of fame and infamy, which he used to entertain and control people, and that was about to turn on him. The engines of his sexuality, theater and self-expression were not powerful enough to combat the emerging unrest of his evolving rivals. Theater and free spiritedness is where he wanted to devote his energy, but some of the Cockettes were sick of his antics and tantrums. As the chasm grew, their anger became palpable.

David Talbot, Author

In his bestselling book, *Season of the Witch,* David documents the antics, tantrums and obstinate behaviors of Hibiscus (the "Divine Dictator") in San Francisco.

Hibiscus created a circle of Magic wherever he went in San Francisco, which had never seen anything quite like the Cockettes. Hibiscus and company broke down all the drag queen traditions. They were not clean-shaven men costumed as women, but all sorts of imaginative – and often furry – creatures. The audience at Cockettes shows "couldn't tell if someone was a man or woman" onstage, marveled filmmaker John Waters, who rode the drag troupe's long, sequined train to notoriety in San Francisco.

He was an angel of light. Wherever he went he dusted the world with glitter and sequins. His lovers, including [Allen] Ginsberg, had to accustom themselves to being glitter encrusted after spending the night with him. "It was difficult to sleep on [his] sheets because there was this sort of like difficult stuff there," recalled the poet. "And it was always in our lips and in our buttholes… You couldn't quite get it out."

But as the Cockettes' star soared higher, Hibiscus resisted the siren call of commercial success. He may have dressed like Monroe and Mansfield, but he didn't want their gilded cage lives. Hibiscus had taken a vow of poverty during his days at the Kaliflower commune, and though he finally moved out of its monastic environment, he was still honoring Irving Rosenthal's "everything free" belief system.

No one was getting rich off The Cockettes success. Sebastian, the late-night impresario at the Palace, charged only $2 a ticket. Each member of the troupe was lucky to earn a few bucks off the shows - "enough to keep us in false eyelashes," as one Cockette put it. But Hibiscus thought even this was too big a concession to Mammon. He wanted the shows to be entirely free. When Sebastian resisted, Hibiscus and his cohorts ran around the theater, flinging open the exit doors to the swarming crowds.

87

John Waters, who would find a way to make a good living off his cultural subversion, never understood Hibiscus's "hippie communism." As time went by, more of the Cockettes began to share Water's view, finding their leader's free philosophy and unpredictable antics increasingly tiresome. Their frustration finally erupted in the summer of 1971, as the troupe pondered traveling east for its big New York stage debut. At an emotional meeting in the second-floor flat of The Cockettes upper Market Street commune, several performers turned on the troupe's founder. Hibiscus was slapped and kicked and pushed down the flight of stairs.

Fayette found him there, at the bottom of the stairwell, in a puddle of tears. He had been violently ejected from his own dream. Fayette thought it was a devastating blow—not only for Hibiscus but also for the entire troupe. "Yes, he had a way-over-the-top personality," she reflected, "but they didn't get it. They didn't want anyone to mess up their make up. My feeling was, 'Please mess it up!' They were ego driven and uninteresting. Hibiscus wanted to do something more fantastical and revolutionary." (3)

Although heartsick, Hibiscus' buoyant spirit rose above the roar. He moved on from The Cockettes and formed a new troupe called The Angels of Light. Ever resilient, Hibiscus launched his new paradigm by acting in Gregory Pickup's film *Pickup's Tricks* (4) in which he played Jesus Christ being crucified. It was filmed at Land's End in San Francisco. Hibiscus carried a large cross down the hill to the shoreline. The cross was staked into the ground and he was fixed to it with ropes. Hibiscus hung there for two hours, his crown of thorns a stinging reminder of all that he had lost – his house, his possessions, his costumes his troupe. Several of the Cockettes, dressed all in black, showed up to play the part of the decadent corrupt priests, calling him names and spitting on him as he hung on the cross – while his Angels of Light looked on adoringly, but helpless to relieve his suffering.

Images from Gregory Pickup's film 'Pickup's Tricks' (1971-1973), featuring Hibiscus and the Angels of Light

Andrew Blauvelt

Artist Gregory Pickup had met Hibiscus while studying filmmaking at the San Francisco Art Institute, and the performer's escapades and shows with The Angels of Light became a central component of his film *Pickup's Tricks.* Shot between 1971 and 1973, the film features various Bacchanalian performances and raucous events at 330 Grove Street, a warehouse-turned-cultural space operated by the African-American empowerment group United Projects; a clean-shaven Allen Ginsberg, in Yiddish Mameh drag, singing from William Blake's Songs of Innocence and Experience; and an Easter reenactment of the Crucifixion at a local beach, among other scenes. Pickup's film offers a rare glimpse into the burgeoning underground queer theater scene of San Francisco in the early 1970s – a heady moment of freewheeling performances, gender-bending personas, and drug-fueled mayhem that emerged in a "post-Haight" environment and that would help give birth to genres such as glitter rock. (4)

Do Lee, Hibiscus' friend and collaborator and Angel Jack's childhood friend

Jack Coe went out to San Francisco from the East Coast in early 1971. I was living on a rainbow commune in Middleburgh, in upstate New York, and made a visit to see my family in SF in the spring. Jack took me to see the Angels of Light Easter pageant at Land's End, with Hibiscus on the cross. Someone he met on the street or in a bar had told him about it.

We hung out on the fringes of this happening and Jack was absolutely smitten by Hibiscus. Soon they were dating. The three of us went for a couple of sunny rides around the city in my mom's convertible, Jack driving, everyone's hair blowing.

When out walking, Hibiscus liked to touch certain things for luck. He loved to pick flowers from anywhere and everywhere. Jack Coe was soon to switch from plaid shirts to sequins... and be named, by Hibiscus, "Angel Jack."

Hibiscus' lover and Angel of Light "Angel Jack" Coe, NYC circa 1979

At that time Hibiscus must have already left Kaliflower commune for the Cockettes. He spoke about Irving, and the regulations of the commune. We went to the Cockette house, briefly, and I remember how nice people were and Jilala showed us stunning Chinese Opera costumes. Also, (I think it was then) Jack and I went to a midnight Cockettes show at the palace, where Divine performed. Years later, Jack, George and I stopped to drop in on John Waters in Baltimore, on our way by bus from NY to Florida. Divine was there and made us spaghetti. He told us that his best tits were made with about a kilo of dry lentil beans.

I soon went back to rural life in Middleburgh, New York, and made one hitchhiking trip to SF. I visited briefly with Jack, he had just gotten over hepatitis, was staying with Rodney and an old guy, a poet/writer like Hart Crane, but what was his name?

Eventually Jack and George came East and came up to Middleburgh for a short visit. That must have been in the fall of 1972. Both in plaid shirts, with long hair and beards... making no waves in the quite straight scene there at the commune. They had left San Francisco for New York City.

PART III
The Angels of Light and the Fairy Tale

*The Angels of Light opened their shows on the full moon. Hibiscus
presented his art free to the public. His art was symbolic of free
expression for all.*

Chapter 6
The Angels of Light - West meets East

The West Coast Angels of Light
– resurrection, transition, evolution ...

*Although heavy hearted about the Cockettes, Hibiscus
founded a new troupe and theater art form called
the Angels of Light. Hibiscus came back with a ROAR!
Photo: Angel Jack (left), Hibiscus (right)
Hibiscus' archives, circa 1972*

The transition from The Cockettes to the Angels of Light was difficult
for Hibiscus. He was still living in San Francisco and trying to come to

terms with being ousted from everything that meant anything to him. Hibiscus was emotionally spent and moody.

He was drawn to people who could facilitate his vision of free theater, free expression and the idea that people should love and have sex with one another. San Francisco's Haight-Ashbury in the 1960s was the perfect environment and paradigm to fully actualize his free-spirited vision and tenacious personality. The 1970s were looming, offering only anxiety-provoking, uncharted scary waters for him to contemplate.

Tahara describes Hibiscus' new way of being; post-Cockettes.

> Irving Rosenthal's commune continued to expand. His newsletter Kaliflower inspired more communes, and there were now hundreds of people in San Francisco living this way. These earth-loving communistic types were to be the audience for the Angels of Light Free Theater.
>
> The communal scene thought of itself as the creator of a new world, a new tribe dedicated to a higher state of human existence, no more wars, no more greed, no more poverty, peace, love. It was a beautiful time to have a free culture, to do theater, to bake, to dance, to share, to have sex, to communicate with each other openly.
>
> Hibiscus found a small theater in downtown San Francisco that would allow his new Angels of Light troupe to do free plays. He wrote a show called *The Moroccan Opera*, an exotic cabaret about Arabic culture with turbans and veils and exotic sets. On an old refrigerator box, Jilala painted a small Arabic screen that stood to one side of the stage.
>
> *The Moroccan Opera* should have been fun but Hibiscus was still too traumatized from losing the Cockettes, who were now becoming even more famous with full houses, celebrities, magazine articles and talk of a New York tour, films, money etc., to be very enthusiastic about this his new group.

94

The West Coast Angels of Light.
Photo: Harris family archives, circa 1972

The first few rehearsals Hibiscus acted as though he were dead, lying on the theater floor motionless staring and speaking to no one. Hibiscus managed to find a few sparks of weak enthusiasm now and then, and we did the show. I do remember several of the Cockettes all dressed in black came to the opening night and booed loudly during the performances several times, and although it was an ugly scene, we knew their intention was to humiliate us.

Allen Ginsberg performing with the Angels of Light (San Francisco)

As time went by, The Angels of Light's audiences became larger, and soon the Angels were considered to be more hip than The Cockettes who now were completely focused on commercial shows with a polished and professional Hollywood look and not as much originality or art.

During summer of 1971 Hibiscus and Allen Ginsberg became lovers. Ginsberg moved into Hibiscus' loft in the

95

Goodman Building and they shared a bed. After a month, Ginsberg went back to New York City.

While in San Francisco, Ginsberg appeared with Hibiscus in The Angels of Light show *Flaming Hot Exotica Erotica*. Ginsberg sang William Blake songs and accompanied himself on his harmonium. After a few successful Angels of Light shows Hibiscus was back.

William Frothingham, aka Palm Spareengz of Seattle's Ze Whiz Kidz, interviewed by W.M. Harris, photos by Chuck Roche.

I first met your brother here in Seattle in the summer 1972. At that point I knew him solely as Hibiscus. At the time I was involved with a group in Seattle called Ze Whiz Kidz, which was very similar to The Cockettes and Angels of Light groups in San Francisco. It was a very organic, like-minded group of friends. We were all involved in the indulgences of the day -

William (Palm) in a Whiz Kidz western parody, "A Fistful of Douchebags"

mainly drugs, sex and rock 'n' roll, spending our days living out old movies, getting dressed up in thrift shop clothing and appearing on the streets.

Seattle at the time was a very small provincial city, and so because of our look and our antics, we were really noticed. It was before the information age, so people here really weren't aware of what was going on anywhere else in the world. Anything arts-related was a really small community here, so everyone knew each other and there were very few degrees of separation. Ze Whiz Kidz started in that environment.

We gave ourselves imaginative, extravagant performing names. Mine, "Palm Spareengz," was really just in my mind. I had never been to the city of Palm Springs, but it evoked something that I thought I wanted to try to re-imagine and express in my performances and my persona.

Communal living was a basic part of the era. We shared several unique houses with exotic names: Savage Gardenias, Hot Ruby's, Lavender Shadows, The Broken Arms, Bedside Manor. It was lots of fun. In those days you could rent a whole house on Capitol Hill for $200 a month, so it was really heaven for creative people at that time. It wasn't a struggle to survive.

A few people had day jobs, but there weren't a lot of career oriented Whiz Kidz! It was a 24-hour job between making appearances, writing the shows and going to the thrift stores and the Public Market where you could find great vintage items from the 20s and 30s for only a quarter. That's where our clothing came from. It was

Ze Whiz Kids of Seattle, early 1970s, Palm Spareeengz sports a top hat.

an idyllic world for creative people, exploring everything from living arrangements to sexuality to what they ate. That's how we operated.

Hibiscus and Tomata du Plenty were friends from their days of working on The Cockettes. It was 1972, probably the biggest year for Ze Whiz Kidz. They had done a big stage show that summer with Alice Cooper at the Paramount Theater. They were the opening act and it was a really successful show.

Tomata du Plenty, who had been performing with Hibiscus and The Cockettes in San Francisco, came to Seattle about 1970 and was the major influence in our group – our Pied Piper.

Our first performance at the Sky River Rock Festival in Satsop, Washington, was extremely loose, not very rehearsed and had one of the world's longest titles. It was like *"Carmen Miranda and The Andrews Sisters Meet The Wizard of Oz."* And the show was really a fiasco, a disaster. The Whiz Kidz had taken way too much LSD and were dropping the microphones on the stage and blowing out the amps. But we were a great hit with the audience because they felt very akin to us. We weren't stars, but we were very glamorous – and, well, people just loved us. There were probably 40 people in that show.

It was huge! Our Gorilla Rose once joked that if there were as many people who claimed to be Whiz Kidz, we'd need a stage as big as China. That was in its infancy. As the group matured, we'd start fleshing out ideas and writing shows on a Thursday, and then we'd perform them on Fridays and Saturday evenings at midnight, in the Smith Tower's basement, The Submarine Room. They were cabaret shows – small scale with lots of skit humor and songs. All we had for music was a battered old upright piano and an old high-school grade turntable and sound system. All rough, but that was the charm. Our piano player, Diva La Lune, was a brilliant musicologist. He just had this incredible knowledge of any kind of show tune and opera, so he brought a great musical level to the Whiz Kidz.

1972 was probably the biggest year for Ze Whiz Kids. We did a big stage show that summer, opening for Alice Cooper at Seattle's 3,000-seat Paramount Theater, packed with Alice's fans and ours. It was one of our biggest shows up to that point and really a successful show.

Later that summer, Hibiscus, Gregory Pickup, Rumi and Fayette all traveled to Seattle and stayed at various Whiz Kidz houses. They were here about a month. Fayette had been in Las Vegas, dressing Bette Midler's first shows there. So when she finished that run she came and stayed for about three months. Tomata had already been here a couple of years. We actually did shows with Hibiscus at the Smith Tower Submarine Room, and cabaret appearances around town.

Palm goes bridal

I was so excited to meet Hibiscus because he was one of the originators – so fun – and by the time he arrived in Seattle he was already a star. It was very exciting for us, being groupies and getting to spend time with your rock star. I think he really loved it up here, partly for the innocence, and because San Francisco was definitely "big city" compared to what it was like in Seattle at that time.

Hibiscus went with us to an old-fashioned drag bar in Pioneer Square called The 614. The performers there were very old school drag. They strictly did mime, and didn't sing – there was no live or original music, but there was recorded music. There was one very serious drag queen out there I think, miming a Judy Garland song or something. Hibiscus had grass skirts on his head and he was rolling around on the floor as this drag queen was trying to do his number. Needless to say we were asked to leave shortly thereafter because we were too irreverent for the scene.

In those days the older gay establishment of Seattle didn't appreciate the Whiz Kidz. It was a generational gap. They found it threatening. Our belief at the time was "put it all out there" with no discretion. It was intentionally outrageous and confrontational – but not mean-spirited. We were just confronting tired morals and ethics.

I remember we used to go swimming in a big lake in the Arboretum. There was a hippie nudist beach down there. Big parts of the lake were thick with lily pads and water lilies. And so there were innumerable performances of Venus arising from the half shell, in the water. There may have been photographs shot at the time, of Hibiscus coming up out of the lake with all of this hair and all this tangle of these water lilies, and singing. Yeah, it was pretty magical. A Botticelli Venus, entertaining the hippies in the lake.

*Hibiscus and Palm Spareeengz entertain children at
Vashon Island Beach, Washington, summer 1972*

Hibiscus and I took a ferry over to Vashon Island one day and it was pretty spontaneous. We went to a beach where there were families and kids hanging out. You know Hibiscus, he was teaching these kids to sing "Can't Help Lovin' That Man of Mine" – and they were loving it! We were all out there singing and dancing. It was just so magical.

After spending time with Hibiscus, I was so impressed because he had theatrical knowledge and training which was unique. No one in the Whiz Kidz had any sort of theatrical tradition – we totally made it up. And no one in the Whiz Kidz could really project [their voices] like someone who's worked in the theater. It was a great gift because it brought something to our performances that really would have been missing. Hibiscus was generous about sharing that knowledge. It was just crazy and fun too, because you didn't necessarily have to be really talented. He would tell you that you were fabulous. Tomata did this too – let you create your own onstage persona and do your thing. They would maybe throw some ideas or suggestions to you, but it was all about freedom and improvisation.

Following a month with Ze Whiz Kidz in Seattle, Hibiscus returned to San Francisco to catch up with his West Coast Angels of Light. Tragedy struck when glue sniffers took over a section of their communal residence, opened all the gas pipes and the house burned to the ground. The Angels lost their home, possessions, costumes, props and confidence. As the house went up in smoke, so went Hibiscus' dream of a California utopia – but once recovered from the initial shock, he interpreted the fire as a sign that it was time to start over.

The East Coast Angels of Light
- There's No Place Like Home!

Michael Varrati: As the Cockettes made a move to a more commercial status, when you and Hibiscus left, was this when the Angels of Light were formed?

> **Rumi:** It was! Hibiscus started the Angels of Light when the Cockettes booted him out. At first, it was a free theater in celebration of essence and beauty, and wasn't a Broadway show tunes kind of thing.

101

For Hibiscus, the fire at the Angels' house was the final blow. Feeling defeated and confused, he and his partner, Angel Jack Coe, relocated to New York City in the winter of 1972. Photo: Harris family archives

When Hibiscus formed the Angels of Light, and subsequently went to New York, what were his feelings in the aftermath? Did he maintain a positive feeling for the Cockettes?

Rumi: When he was booted out, he was done with it. When he went to New York, he started a second contingent of the Angels family. I left San Francisco in late 71 or 72, and I went and worked with a group called Ze Whiz Kids, which was kind of an offshoot of the Cockettes. I was living in Montreal, Canada…and the whole time I was just waiting for Hibiscus to call and say, "Come to New York!" Ultimately, I did and I worked with Hibiscus, his family, and the Angels of Light in New York. (1)

Once Angel Jack and Hibiscus stepped across the threshold of his boyhood apartment in the East Village of New York City, life was never the same for anyone. His sisters answered the front door and beheld the bejeweled, glitter-bearded, gender-bended duo that had just arrived from San Francisco. Hibiscus brought home a new art form. His family welcomed him and his lover with open arms. The Harris family joined the circus and never looked back.

Hibiscus, now age 23, enlisted his sisters, Jayne Anne, Eloise and Mary Lou, his brother Fred Harris, and his mother Ann, to bring their seasoned theatrical skills to Hibiscus' new ventures. His brother Walter Michael had already settled out west, having found his own version of a California utopia in a semi-monastic, new age religious community.

Ann Harris became Hibiscus' songwriter, co-performer and confidant. Being a creative writer and poet, Ann began the most prolific time in her songwriting career with the Angels of Light.

Hibiscus' sisters had forgotten all the teasing their brother had put them through when they were young. They were happy he was home and could give them a break from the round-the-clock monotony of off-off Broadway … theater, school, theater … repeat, repeat, repeat. But the young Harris girls did not bank on Angel Jack coming into the mix.

(clockwise from left) Ann, Jayne Anne, Mary Lou and Eloise Harris in this Andrew Sherwood portrait from the mid-1960s

Photos by Andrew Sherwood: Hibiscus' sisters: L.to R. Jayne Anne, Mary Lou (both photos) in the Angels of Light at TNC, 1972

A-Crystal Field B-George Bartenieff C-Ann Harris D-George III E-Mary Lou Harris F-George III G-Angel Jack Coe H-Carolyn Graham I-Rocky Roads J-Eloise Harris K-Chuck Dancer L-Billy Rafferty M-Jayne Anne Harris: *Sky High*, Book/George III, Music and Lyrics/ Ann, Theater for the New City, 1972 or 73.

Hibiscus was fun, magical and glamorous when interacting with his sisters. Angel Jack, however, although colorful and loving in his own way, had a toxic tongue. No matter what Jayne Anne, Eloise or Mary Lou would say or do, Angel Jack would free associate sexual imagery. He would say things like, "Oh Honey, I'd like to lick his lollipop," or sing "Ooh, honey, gray skies are gonna clear up, if you sit on a happy face." This occured in front of friends and sometimes teachers. Nevertheless, the family was very excited and felt blessed to have Hibiscus back home and ready to begin a new exciting and creative adventure.

But first Hibiscus had to deal with a pressing and catastrophic issue. The new, "commercial" Cockettes had come to New York to perform at The Anderson Theater in the East Village (only blocks away from Hibiscus' family apartment). The media rolled out the red carpet. Truman Capote and Rex Reed, who had seen them in San Francisco and experienced their euphoric tribal feeling, came back to the Big Apple to trumpet their glory to New York's high society and the highbrow theatrical world. The "new" Cockettes tried to appropriate Hibiscus' image for their branding on posters in front of the Anderson Theater. Incensed, Ann stormed over to the theater and demanded that the management immediately remove the posters. When they refused, she ripped them down herself.

New York Times Style Section, November 9, 1971,
Excerpt from: *The Cockettes: The Show Was a Drag…*

> What had been "gay, light and campy" in San Francisco, became boring, tedious, tasteless, stupid and amateurish in New York and the audience begin walking out in droves after the first two hours of the nearly endless four-hour fiasco. The sound was inaudible, the cues were missed, the props were lost, the ad-libs were omitted, and a whole new Gotham City routine was added for the benefit of the audience who had come to see the San Francisco show. "My God, this is worse than Hiroshima," cried Rex Reed, who had given them a glowing review from San Francisco. "Truman Capote would have died." (2)

Fueled by the schadenfreude that the Cockettes had bombed on his home turf, plus returning to his roots and family, Hibiscus' positive energy returned. It took him no time to recruit an East Coast Angels of Light theater troupe and infuse it with his glitter, extravagance and magic. This time around he let his family members become creative partners as well as performers. His parents and siblings had spent the last decade performing on and off Broadway, in repertory companies, in films, and on television and radio in New York, and were well seasoned for this new adventure.

Hibiscus in the Angels of Light, NYC, circa 1972, family archive

Ann and George Harris, Sr. are considered pioneers in off-off-Broadway theater and performance art. Photo by Sheyla Baykal

Ann especially welcomed the return of her wandering son George. With his encouragement, Ann wrote music and lyrics for a multitude of full length shows performed by Hibiscus' Angels of Light in New York, the Netherlands, Germany, Paris, San Francisco and Provincetown on Cape Cod. She is rumored to have taught every queen in Greenwich Village to tap dance during the East Coast Angels of Light period. Ann's powerful showbiz prowess didn't stop at songwriting. She spent well over a decade performing off-off-Broadway and in summer stock. As an actress she was a favorite of playwrights Lanford Wilson and Harry Koutoukas—the latter bestowing upon her his highest honorific … "a gargoyle."

Left to right: Jayne Anne, Ann, Mary Lou and Eloise Harris performing the Military Tap in Enchanted Miracle, *the Angels of Light at Theater for the New City. Photo: Andrew Sherwood, 1972*

The Harris family was hard at work in the experimental off-off Broadway and counter-culture scenes in New York City. Ann and/or her daughters performed frequently at The New York Shakespeare Festival Public Theater, The Caffe Cino, La MaMa ETC, Judson Poets Theater and Theater for the New City. George Sr. landed a plum role in Broadway's *The Great White Hope* and continued with the show's national tour after the Broadway run. Returning, he performed with the Angels of Light when his schedule permitted. Ann played Doris Acker in the cult film, *The Honeymoon Killers.* Walter Michael contributed ideas and music from out West, and brother Fred designed lights for many off-off-Broadway productions, while arranging and playing Ann's songs for Hibiscus' shows.

All of these artistic blessings were more than the family could ask for, but something was missing – time and attention toward development of the younger kids. They needed a decent bedtime, time to do their homework, encouragement and breathing room for their own ideas and growing interests. The Harris household was well versed in child tantrums that would arise when any one of them was feeling overwhelmed or ignored. George's tantrums were the biggest and the loudest. It wasn't a surprise that his voice and ideas dominated the spotlight in the Harris dwelling.

Michael Varrati interview, continued:

> **Rumi:** I always admired him, because the Cockettes weren't about doing runs of shows, night after night. We would do something once, twice and then putting it away to do something else. But, we did this Angels of Light show in New York in 1972 called "The Enchanted Miracle." The show was based on this comet that was going to pass over the Earth, which was supposed to be visible to the naked eye, but fizzled out and never did. Hibiscus wanted to do a run of two free shows a night based around this event, for two months. Completely free to the public. He would pick up people off the street and put them in the show. It was incredible how it all came together, and it's an experience of which I'm really proud. It was magic.
>
> Being free to the people of New York was really a plus, because everyone came. All my idols—Warhol, Alejandro Jodoworsky—they all came to the show. The theater was filled to capacity every night. It was wonderful. (1)

Angels of Light shows began with a glittering sunrise in which Hibiscus played Apollo. At Theater for the New City (NYC) Photo by Andrew Sherwood, 1972

The Angels of Light's shift from the West Coast to the East resulted in an interesting mixture of cast members, theater rituals and life styles, which reimagined the idea that gay, straight, male, female, mother, father, sibling or friend of all ages, colors and talents could thrive together as a tribe (or troupe). Photo: courtesy of David Loehr, Angels of Light, Theater for the New City, 1972

The New York Angels of Light portrayed Hibiscus new vision of utopia. The musicals encompassed epic themes including the dawning of time, the Garden of Eden, good versus evil, human evolution, ancient and contemporary civilizations and heaven itself. These "history of everything" themes demanded the grandest of sets and costumes, choral harmonies and epic dance and tap sequences *á la* Busby Berkeley. Hibiscus' new scripts afforded solo turns in which individual cast members could demonstrate their impressive skills and shine their brightest light. Perhaps being back in New York City inspired Hibiscus to write with a broader brush. Nevertheless, he held fast to his ethic of free theater, which meant low budgets and lots of volunteers.

John Edward Heys acted with Cookie Mueller, H.M. Koutoukas, Charles Ludlam, Ethyl Eichleberger and the Angels of Light NYC. Abridged BOMB Magazine interview.

Photo by Peter Hujar

Just a note about how I became involved with The New York City Angels of Light. I had met Hibiscus after he left the first Cockette House on lower Haight St. on my first trip to S.F. in 71. I was staying with Grasshopper further up on Haight St. with many other tenants, guests, drop-ins, etc. Around the corner was The Kaliflower House, which Irving Rosenthal ruled, no shoes allowed in the house nor toilet paper. I honestly don't recall if Hibiscus resided there. Tahara did, and Shalala, amongst others. Harlow and others remained at The Cockette House on Oak St. which housed Sweet Pam, Scrumbly, Link, Marshall, and John Flowers, with occasional guests such as myself. That was my favorite place to live on my total of three trips. I guess the split had pretty much divided people, and I can't recall seeing Hibiscus much.

My other favorite house was on DuBoce St, the last house abutting a park, which housed Adrian Milton, Grasshopper, and I cannot recall who else. Dicken Acramen and Hibiscus made formal visits.

Back in NYC, Hibiscus and Jack (I have no idea how he appeared on the scene) had settled in NYC. Where? Have no idea but long before the Co-op in the West Village. I had my first East Village flat at 315 E. 6th St, & arrived home one late afternoon to find a note wedged in my door roughly saying "Hi John, Jack and I would love for you to be in the first New York City Angels of Light show, titled *Springtime Extravaganza.*" The show consisted of Jack Tree, Zamba Gomez and myself. We performed for one weekend in long swaths of glittered dark purple synthetic like silk or taffeta, swaying back and forth intoning "WE ARE THE DARK CLOUDS OF THE NIGHT," a constant refrain of that same lyric. The show was in Leandro Katz's top floor loft on East 4th St, and somehow we packed them in, but honestly, how? We were all so stoned (I speak for myself and my two fellow performers). Somehow I have deja vu that Hibiscus forbade any kind of drugs, so as long as we followed this rather threadbare script...all went smooth. (3)

Do Lee

When I left the commune in 1973 and was at loose ends in Manhattan, I found Angel Jack and Hibiscus temporarily crashing at a friend's tiny East Village apartment. Was his name Randy? If it was, it sure fit. He had these metal rings hanging on lines from the ceiling (I didn't know they were cock rings until Jack told me.) Hibiscus was very entertaining and kept everyone's spirits up! It was a pretty claustrophobic environment. I think I stayed a night on the couch.

Bars, the Baths, cruising, hustling...there was a frantic lot going on, New York City was a real pressure cooker. I was very naïve, and Jack clued me in on a lot about queer life. Hibiscus was always nice to me, and, although I wasn't exactly familiar

111

with a lot of his world of nostalgia, musicals, divas etc., I was glad to join in when they needed help backstage at an Angels of Light Show at the Theater for the New City, down on Jane Street in the West Village. I loved theater all my life and had given up trying to act early on, at about 12, when I blew my lines as the Judge in a play about Sacco and Vanzetti. So I had had some experience with stage managing, and had done a summer internship in the prop room at A.C.T. in San Francisco. Off-off Broadway was thrilling, those were wonderful times, going to rehearsals, getting to know the Harris family, and being part of the shows. I was good with helping the chorus with the mad rush of costume and headdress changes, getting shredded by glitter, frantically pinning up ripped dresses. I learned to do the white face and rhinestone makeup and sometimes helped Hibiscus get made up. He could be very sweet and appreciative when he wanted to be and really win people's hearts.

Hibiscus was welcomed back into the New York theater scene with open arms. Crystal Field and George Bartinieff, co-founders of Theater for the New City, gave him and his new troupe a permanent theatrical home on Jane Street in the West Village. Performers far and wide flocked to be part of a Hibiscus extravaganza. Unlike the meat-grinding review that the "new" Cockettes (without Hibiscus) received upon their New York debut, Hibiscus and his Angels of Light were well received, well loved and well documented by the press.

After Dark Magazine, excerpt from *On High with the Angels of Light* by Henry Edwards, August 1973

Drenched in glitter, they prance down the shabby streets of New York, an iridescent reminder that oppressive living conditions need not rob man of his ability to express himself imaginatively. They appear at the door, they are ushered in, and then suddenly take on a celestial glow that proves that these two young men can charge any environment that is adaptable to assuming new life. They are Hibiscus and Jack, the Angels of Light, and they have thus far staged three multi-set, multi costume Technicolor extravaganzas on the tiny stage of the charming Theater for a New City on New York City's lower west side, a few short blocks from the Hudson River. The Angels do not charge an admission fee; they never play to an empty seat; their audiences, aware of these conditions, arrive at least an hour before the performance and even seem to enjoy the wait. A communal sense of expectancy sweeps this crowd. Merely the anticipation of the Angels' joyful ability to enchant and their humanistic point of view is enough to unite a room filled with strangers. (4)

Hibiscus' shows always opened on a full moon. He did the writing and starring and Angel Jack made the costumes and sets and probably managed the worrisome budget. In New York, Hibiscus earned the level of popularity that he enjoyed on the West Coast. Famous people were beginning to appear in the audience. The guest list included the Osmond family, The Rolling Stones, John and Yoko, David Bowie and independent filmmaker Shirley Clarke.

Hibiscus wrote and performed social satire, scenarios that had everything to do with freedom of expression, freedom to be gay (and happy), and the power of love – yet had nothing intentionally to do with sexuality. His New York Angels of Light shows – *Gossamer Wings*, *Enchanted Miracle* and the *Birdie Follies* – featured archetypal qualities and characters: Mother Nature, animals, planets, gods and goddesses, love, hate, mythology,

Hibiscus and Angel Jack
Photo by David Loehr, 1972

historical events and God and the Devil, playing out the history of the world with all of its triumphs and disasters. Hibiscus art was not "drag," though writers often describe it with that misleading label. "Gender-bending" was a conscious element of his theatrical palette, but his aim was to adorn who *you* were – gay, straight, or otherwise. More apt descriptors of his art are *magical, organic, glittering.* It was visually beautiful and yes, campy at times – but never bathed in overtly sexual tones. Hibiscus' Angels of Light musicals celebrated human relationships and life scenarios that have played repeatedly throughout the arts going back centuries.

Tim Robbins
Family friend and Oscar-winning actor, writer, and director

I don't know how it was that I wound up in a vortex of the culture that would later define us all.

I ran spotlight at the Theater for the New City in the early 1970s for a show called the Angels of Light. I was 13 years old and the reason I was there was that I had a crush on Eloise Harris, an angel in her own right, and sister of George Harris Jr. who I knew as Hibiscus, the creative force of this troupe of freaks and weirdos that were making theatrical magic in Greenwich Village with their combination of glitter and outrageous talent. It would be disingenuous to compare the Angels of Light to anything within our modern perceptions of entertainment because they created the mold.

They were doing things in the 1970s that had not been done before. No one had lived as large in the utter joy of free expression as the Angels. They brought it like rock stars. What they were bringing was a beautiful combination of 1930's Hollywood musical numbers, a camp before there was a camp sensibility and a radical commitment to a new form of entertainment fueled by an extreme pride in an alternative sexuality. Add in a little LSD and a lot of glitter and imagine the minds being blown and expanded in the audiences that were lucky enough to see them live. And there I was present behind my spotlight at 13 years old witnessing this spectacle.

We all think of Greenwich Village, in retrospect, as a place where this would naturally happen but those of us that lived there during this time know that it was more complicated than that. The village for all its progressive thought and free thinking inhabitants was also surrounded by old world thinking, conservative strains that resisted the freaks and the weirdos, second and third-generation Italian and Irish that saw the Angels and all these other hippies as a threat upon their catholic sensibilities and upon their own conceptions of sexuality. In other words, it wasn't a safe or easy thing to do, even in Greenwich Village, to dress in glitter drag and to own one's homosexuality. It was, in fact, a radical act, not for the faint of heart. This flaunt hadn't been done before in such a brash and prideful way. To produce this kind of theater one needed real men, the kind of men that had real balls, the kind of man that would walk up to a soldier and place a flower in the barrel of a loaded gun.

I remember being intimidated by Hibiscus and Jack and by the other members of this wild company. I was a jock at the time and the intimidation didn't come from a fear that they would hurt me. The intimidation came from a feeling that these were fiercely committed individuals that had determined their path, a path I did not understand at the time. They were on the road of freedom with full knowledge of the dangers that lay ahead. They owned every inch of who they were and were not waiting to be legitimized by me or society or law. They were singing out and singing loud and they were kicking ass theatrically. All those that followed in their wake owe a huge debt of gratitude to Hibiscus, the Angels of Light and the Harris family.

Anyone that has, in the last 50 years defied societal expectations, pushed the envelope of sexuality, or lived courageously in the freedom of their skin should say a prayer of thanks, light a candle and line their eyes with glitter for George Jr. and the Harrises of Greenwich Village. (5)

Left to right: Chuck Dancer (Sugar), Hibiscus, Angel Jack and Zomba in Enchanted Miracle. *Sheyla Bakyal photo, circa 1972*

Photo collage of the Harris family in a variety of shows during the 1960s and 70s, created by Patricia Mansfield Harris

Adrian Milton

By this time Hibiscus had left the Cockettes and started the Angels of Light. I was more attuned to the free theater vibe and when Hibiscus asked me if I wanted to be an Angel, I said yes.

The poster that reads HIBISCUS Productions presents ANGELS OF LIGHT, FREE, Holiday Gala Pageant (and is marked in the bottom, lower left as "The Last Show"), etc....is, if I am not mistaken the last show that Hibiscus did. [It was not - *Tinsel Town Tirade* was his last – Ed.] The cast included Hibiscus, Jack, Ann, the three sisters, Beauregard, myself, and a musician. (There may have been one or two more people in the cast but I really cannot remember. Jack might). The show was held at the Washington Square Methodist Church on West Fourth Street in NYC. The scant, last minute promotion drew fewer than twenty people in the audience. Beauregard played all of the Three Kings. The show featured Hibiscus, Jack and his three sisters in their larger than life glitterama costumes. I don't remember what Beau and I did besides float around and join in the singing of the Christmas carols. The whole tone of the show had a rather melancholy, bittersweet quality. So few people showed up. It really did seem like the Final Curtain, the end of an era. Hibiscus realized this and said something to this effect to me: "Well, Honey, we gave it our best shot and it was fun while it lasted." He was in a very philosophical mood. We all exited into the chill night air, a little snow falling, and sang (carols) on our way down the streets.

David Loehr, New York Angel of Light

I grew up in Pittsfield, Massachusetts. After graduating from high school in 1967 I moved to New York and attended Parson's School of Design and the Lester Polokov School of Theater Design where I learned set painting and set building.

During that time I met a mystical fellow named Emilio Mercado who had a two-story apartment at 163 W. 10th Street at 7ᵗʰ Avenue, where a group of people lived communal style, including Billy Rafford. The apartment was adorned with fabrics, feathers, glitter, tassels, flowers and an array of art, paintings and assemblages. It was my first glimpse of the gay, hippie, free love lifestyle.

I moved back to Massachusetts into a small shack in the woods in Hinsdale for two years with no electricity or running water, and frequently took the bus or hitchhiked back and forth to New York and stayed with Emilio at apartments at 20 Renwick Street and 86 Perry Street.

Hibiscus back-left, Emilio with umbrella, Chuck Dancer aka Sugar front-left. Photo: David Loehr, Angels of Light at TNC 1972

On one trip to the city in 1972 Emilio took me to a rehearsal of an Angels of Light upcoming production of *Gossamer Wings* at Theater for The New City on Jane Street. Emilio was in the show along with Billy Rafford and another close friend whom I had met at Max's Kansas City a year earlier named Rocky Roads. I don't recall quite how it happened but before I knew it I was participating in— and became a performer in—several of the musical numbers in the spectacular production. In one of the numbers, "Bombay Baby," Emilio played Krishna and was covered in blue makeup, beads and a gold hat. One evening he wasn't able to make the performance so I took his role as Krishna on that night.

It was a very exciting time and the cast of characters was amazing, especially Hibiscus who took a liking to me and was

118

always just so sweet and caring. We got along like old friends from the beginning. Others from the cast that I remember and stayed friends with were Zamba, Charles Angel, Moulty, and Roy Allen.

Do Lee

Angel Jack and Hibiscus were looking for investors to help build a new show, and I got them together with my dad and Ed O'Rourke, who had been his colleague in the Agency for International Development in the 1960s. We went to Ratner's Dairy Restaurant and had a hilarious dinner with blintzes and knishes – Hibiscus really charmed them and they put up $3,000. With this money, Jack bought cardboard, glue, glitter, sequined fabric and rented a loft on 2nd Avenue (cheap, there was no glass in the big window on the street.) We lived and worked there, building the show that eventually won top prize for the Angels of Light Free Theater at the Holland Festival. Then they took the show to Paris, to the ill-fated venue Theatre de Campaigne Premier.

Hibiscus was often in a lot of pain during that winter on 2nd Avenue. He had bone spurs in his legs. And I think he had symptoms of advanced syphilis also. The room he and Jack had was cheerful and cozy, but we had no heat in the place and he was in bed a lot. He did lots of PR, sent charming cards to people, and kept up the beautiful scrapbook (which I think Jack might have had after Hibiscus died and it disappeared after Jack died.) Jack was determined that we could be healthy on a miniscule budget, had figured out how three people could survive on something like $3 a day: one Dannon yogurt with fruit, raw spinach and a dense, whole grain (maybe sprouted, certainly no yeast) bread from the baker boys down on 6th St. I would go to the 24-hour Korean vegetable stand to get spinach, sometimes in the middle of the night, we felt very safe. Hibiscus liked to flirt with the baker boys so he would go get the bread. Living and working with them, I got some idea of the jealousy they fueled in each other. Both of them could put on big dramas. Jack hustled, so we usually had some hash to smoke, and that would smooth things over. There was plenty of work to do, making big glitter backdrops, dozens of headdresses and stretch sequin dresses.

Hibiscus read a lot and I remember him talking about the novel *Mandingo* on that trip. Stopping in Baltimore to see John Waters was a big highlight for me, and the fresh grapefruit in Florida, right off the tree, was fantastic.

We took a bus trip to Florida, to see a friend of Hibiscus' who was going to do a photo shoot at the beach. Photo: Do Lee, circa 1973

Hibiscus liked to put iodine in baby oil and baste himself with that and roast on the beach. He said it would make him tan faster. The beach photo shoot was ok, we probably said then O, Fabulous! Mermaids...But I don't know if the pictures ever got used. Back in New York, I took a picture, using a star-point lens, of Angel Jack and Hibiscus in rhinestone makeup with glitter beards, and it made the cover of The Advocate in San Francisco.

David Loehr

In April of 1974 The Angels took part in the premiere of the film *Ladies and Gentlemen... The Rolling Stones* at The Ziegfeld Theater on East 54th Street. I was supposed to be one of The Angels who ran up and down the theater's aisles throwing styrofoam frisbees with the Sticky Fingers tongue on them into the audience along with Angel Jack, Hibiscus, the Harris sisters and others. Unfortunately, the number of Angels needed for the event was cut back and I was bumped from the event.

Shortly afterwards, in June of 1974, I moved into the big house on Main Street in Tannersville, New York, which had formerly been an Inn, with Jack, Hibiscus, Rumi Missabu and a couple of others. There were plans for a European tour and we were all there building sets, rehearsing and planning the shows. As it turned out, only a few Angels went to Europe, perhaps only Jack and Hibiscus. Once there, they recruited new people to perform in the shows.

The stay in Tannersville had some rocky moments. Jack and Hibiscus were seeing a guy named Robert who lived with them at the time, which created a great deal of tension. I remember one evening Hibiscus came running into my room on the third floor of the house scared and cowering because he had caught Jack and Robert in bed without him and tossed a bucket of water on them. He was terrified and I got the impression that Jack had been abusive to him. There was a lot of yelling and screaming in the house that night.

During my stay in Tannersville I got a job at Villagio Italia, a nearby resort, working in the kitchen to make money for the rent and food. It was an interesting job and got me out of the house for a while. Kaaterskill Falls was also nearby, which proved to be a peaceful and beautiful getaway.

Lake Rip Van Winkle was within a short walking distance from the house. One day Hibiscus and I walked to the lake and in the passion of the moment we spontaneously stripped naked in a wide-open field in the warm sun and made love for the first and only time.

Shortly afterward I hit the road and left Tannersville to travel around the country seeing many of David Bowie's *Diamond Dogs* Tour concert dates.

Later on, I would occasionally run into Hibiscus around New York and we were always so happy to see each other. I remained close with Emilio Mercado, Billy Rafford, Roy Allen and Rocky Roads, all of whom, including Hibiscus, would die from the AIDS scourge except Roy, who was killed in an automobile accident on the Long Island Expressway.

When Emilio died in 1991 I basically inherited many of his belongings from his Renwick Street apartment, which I had the key to since 1968. I took several vanloads of belongings out before the landlord threw everything out to the street, which eventually did happen to what was left behind.

Among the treasures that I rescued were eighty color transparencies from the Gossamer Wings production. Emilio was a close friend with the photographer Peter Hujar, who attended several of the shows. I've always wondered if the photos may have been taken by Peter because of their high quality. I still have a glittered cardboard star from the backdrop of Gossamer Wings, which I cherish. It was a magical time and my memories of Hibiscus and The Angels of Light are wonderful.

Hibiscus could make an audience laugh, howl and cry with his talented troupe of ballet dancers, torch-song singers, children and tap dancers galore. Each one brought his or her special gifts to the shows. Angel Jack dressed them and Hibiscus matched them to movement and music. They spent tons of time on their costumes; less so on rehearsal.

Ann continued to support Hibiscus' experiments, artistic endeavors and theatrical productions to the point of excluding the initiatives of her other children. The unspoken family mantra was to follow and support the golden boy or be doomed, ignored, teased and dished incessantly. George had so many theatrical and artistic projects going at one time that there was little time, space or oxygen left in the room for anyone else's ideas.

122

That said, Hibiscus nurtured and gave a platform to an array of artistic and activist voices. For example, there was "Miss Marsha," a guest performer with the Angels of Light—and more:

A determined street activist and organizer for ACT-UP – AIDS Coalition to Unleash Power and co-founder of STAR – Street Transvestite Action Revolutionaries, **Marsha P. Johnson** fought vehemently for gay liberation. She worked tirelessly to help other young trans kids find clothing, food and shelter. She was identified as one of the first to fight back at the famous Stonewall Riots in 1969. (6)

"Miss Marsha"

On stage with the Angels of Light, Miss Marsha was met with standing ovations upon her entrance without ever singing a note or dancing a step. She would inevitably break the fourth wall and start talking to the audience, which whipped them into a frenzied back-and-forth banter leading to another standing ovation. Hibiscus eventually stopped assigning songs and dances to Miss Marsha because she rarely got to them. Just being Miss Marsha P. (Pay it No Mind) Johnson was enough magic to electrify the audience.

Hibiscus was a maniacal manifestor who created one extravaganza after another. He could be selfish, but also used his innate gifts for others. His family felt privileged to have a front row seat to the most amazing talents of the parade of costumed boys. Little did they know that these living figures were pioneers of gay free expression who were standing up for the rights of many artists and their LGBTQ brethren.

Bambi Lake in Femme Fatale: The Shocking Pink Life of Jayne Champagne. *Photo: Dan Nicoletta, 1977*

Hibiscus' family witnessed him with glitter in his beard, wearing Kabuki Opera robes with a twelve-foot wingspan, singing excerpts from Puccini's *Madame Butterfly;* Holly Woodlawn, crying real tears on stage, acting and singing her heart out in *Tinsel Town Tirade;* John Rothermel, delivering a heart-wrenching version of "When Your Lover has Gone" in a beaded cocktail dress complete with a feather collar and rhinestone pumps; Java Jet, who later became Bambi Lake, standing well over six-feet-tall in her stiletto heels, with her white goose marabou stole, singing Marilyn Monroe's hit, "Kiss Me;" Chuck Dancer, who would later re-name herself Sugar in *Romy Haag's Drag Burlesque,* dancing on toe shoes in Berlin, as the clown Pierrot, with all the technique and strength of a seasoned ballerina; and the great protector Marsha P. Johnson, a delicate Angel of Light on stage, but a force to be reckoned with when provoked or while looking after the theater kids off-stage. And of course, the magnificent Richard Goldberger, elegantly dancing his Martha Graham American Flag modern art piece in Larry Ray's *Trockadero de Monte Carlo* dance troupe. There were so many gorgeous girls and boys who showed up at the theater looking natural (beautiful, but conventional) and transform themselves into magical sparkling characters who lit up the stage and mesmerized the audience.

The Angels Of Light at Theater For the New City
New York City, 1972

The Angels of Light were blessed with cast members Zomba, Rocky Roades, David Loehr, Marsha P. Johnson, Crystal Field, George Bartenieff, Alexander Bartenieff, Risa Scobie, Julie Carmen, Michael Moore, Chuck Dancer, Johnny Dancer, Sandi, Sandt Litchfield, Carolyn Graham, Brucie Flowers, Eric Bluebird, Billy Rafford, Emilio, Hibiscus, Angel Jack, the Harris family and many more. Photo: Sheyla Baykal, 1972

*Angels of Light cast members: clockwise, from top left: Zomba,
David Loehr, Rocky Roades, Eric Bluebird and Jeri. Sheyla Baykal
photos, The Angels of Light, Theater for the New City, NYC, 1973*

Shelley Valfer
Cast member and stage manager
of the Angels of Light

Angels Of Light and me...

It was the summer of 1973 and I
was right out of college. I had
entered college going for a
degree in Applied Mathematics
but by the end of the four years, I had switched my major to
theater, which was always my first love. I had written, directed
and starred in two one-act plays that were not condoned by the
theater department there. (This is the defunct Bronx campus of
NYU) I managed to get my plays done in the student cafeteria
or dormitory lounge, so I guess you could say I was already
primed for alternative theater. But even that could not have
prepared me for what was about to happen.

I was a full-fledged anti-war protesting hippie. I was no
stranger to gay rights in spite of the fact that I was straight.
During an anti-war protest in Washington where the theme was
"fill the jails" I was locked up in a small county jail cell, 14 to
every one-man cell and among us were a group of homosexual
activists. We held hands through the bars just to give us
strength and courage. And shared cigarettes and bologna
sandwiches on white bread. We filled the jails all right. I forget
what the point of that was, but alas I digress...

I had been to the Theater for the New City as an audience
member in the past and I knew that they were known for their
alternative theater productions and non-mainstream aesthetic.
So I figured, what the hell, I'll just go in and ask for a job.
How hard could it be? I went on a sunny afternoon. I didn't
realize that nobody in the theater gets out of bed before 4:00
p.m. The theater was completely empty and I remember just
being able to walk right in and look around. At this time TNC
was located in what was once the ballroom of a Swedish

127

Seaman's Hotel on Jane and West Street in Greenwich Village. It had become so dilapidated and run down that it was now an SRO for welfare recipients and derelicts. I heard the sound of someone sweeping in the back of the theater. There was George Bartenieff who, with his wife Crystal Field, ran the theater. I don't think I knew who he was at the time and maybe I thought he was just the janitor. I told him that I really wanted to work in the theater and would he please help me to see if I could get a job there. As I recall, the encounter was brief and to the point. "Can you come back tonight? We need an assistant stage manager for the show. Be here at 7:00."

I had no idea what the show was or what I would be doing, but who cared, I was working in the theater. I came back that night and could not believe my eyes. Backstage was filled with big husky bearded guys with very little clothes or flowing silk robes, covered in makeup and glitter. One guy with extremely long bright copper-red hair had a banana stuck in his very tight skimpy underwear. The sets were made out of huge sheets of cardboard that opened like a book to create the backdrop for each of the scenes. This was The Angels of Light presenting *"Gossamer Wings."* The leaders of this impressive bunch were Hibiscus and Angel Jack and they couldn't be more welcoming. I didn't know what I was doing, and nobody would tell me, but eventually I made myself useful either handing out costumes or moving props. Whatever was necessary. One night one of the older gentlemen in the company asked me why I didn't join in the fun. I said, "Well, I don't have a part. What can I do?" He said, "Just throw on a shmata and get on stage." I found a costume that covered my entire body so I couldn't be seen. I think it was a caterpillar of some sort with fabric and metal hoops. I hopped on stage at one of the crazy dance numbers and just wiggled and twirled. What a blast! I was on stage! Performing! In front of a live audience. And boy, were they alive! They whooped and hollered. Some of the audience members were even better dressed than the ones on stage, but none more opulent and impressive than Hibiscus and Angel Jack who changed their costumes multiple times during the show.

128

I remember one in particular who was a favorite among the crowd. He came every night on roller-skates and skated all around the audience. The theater, as I said, used to be a ballroom and the floor was marble. There was a wraparound balcony with a wrought iron rail that stretched a full 180 degrees around the theater. Over time there had been some changes to the space, including the installation of a bathroom on one end of the room. The balcony reached all the way around so it was above the bathroom and was walled off from the rest of the space. This tiny piece of balcony had just enough room for a mattress and was the home of one of the crewmembers at the theater. It became a private lounge that was utilized by the crewmember and myself and others when we needed a little respite from all the craziness going on below. But I'll never forget the smell of piss coming from the men's room below. Ugh. But in some ways, it was my home away from home.

I can't remember how many weeks the show ran but when it was done, I had become a member of the Theater for the New City company, appearing in many shows and musicals. I even got to write and perform a full-length musical of my own there. During this time, Crystal [Field] had written a musical version of *The Little Prince,* which I appeared in playing the fox. It was quite notable because the part of the Little Prince was played by a 13-year-old Tim Robbins. Also in the cast were the amazing Harris sisters, George Harris' (aka Hibiscus) real-life sisters. The Harris sisters, along with their mother, a hoofer par excellence, were the only women who appeared in *Gossamer Wings.* They were so wonderful to work with. I actually hired them to record a demo track for another musical that I was writing years later. They ranged in age at that time from (I think) 8 to 13 or thereabouts. They could sing, they could dance and they were born troupers.

Not long after that, TNC was asked to perform a production of Mario Fratti's, *Chile '73* in Italy. This would be my first ever trip to Europe. We played the International Student Theater Festival in Parma, Italy. It was an eight-day festival but when it was over, me and my friend (the one who's crib was above the men's room) decided to stay and not return to NY. I ended up spending eight months in Europe and it is during that time that I met up with Robert Wilson's company and we performed in Spoleto, Paris, Belgrade and Zurich among others. By now, I guess I had acquired a talent for weaseling my way into a show. All this because I got up the nerve to volunteer myself for a spot as a dancing caterpillar. I owe it all to the Angels of Light.

Ilka Scobie
Mother of Risa – the youngest (age 3) cast member of the New York Angels of Light

Hibiscus Harris and the Angels of Light

Hibiscus came into my life when I was a young mother living in Brooklyn. I'd been hearing about him for a while – he was a great friend and old theatrical pal of my friend Claudia Tedesco [Colmer], who had lived with him in a San Francisco commune.

I knew he was very gorgeous, very gay, and very talented – from a bohemian theatrical family and that he was a founder of the legendary Cockettes, and later the Angels of Light. I think Claudia and her friend Aubrey first brought Hibiscus over to my apartment. He arrived with his boyfriend Angel Jack. Both had long flowing locks and wild beards but Hibiscus' leonine grace really set him apart. They were in New York putting together a production with the Angels of Light, a prescient rebranding.

My three-year-old daughter and then husband were immediately recruited for the show – as was a friend, Rene Adler, who could sing, and her boyfriend, who could strum a guitar. Rehearsals took place at the cavernous old Jane Street theater, near the West Side Highway. What a ragtag troupe – Marsha P. Johnson, the black drag queen and street saint, Rumi

Missabu from California who eventually became my roommate, Brucie Flowermaker the creator of enormous paper blooms, Matt, an older Christopher Street denizen, Andy Laurie, and Do, an old friend of Angel Jack's who became one of their costume makers and devoted groupie. Emilio Cuberio, also in the cast, became an early punk performance artist and a dear friend for a couple of decades.

Hibiscus had three glamorous younger sisters who actually were professional performers, plus the charming Ann Harris, mother, actress, and collaborator. So the cast ranged from serious theater people to delusional drag queens. Throw in recreational drugs, pounds of glitter and glue, camped and amped up old timey musical scores rewritten with wit and performed with endless enthusiasm. Crystal Field and George Bartenieff were also involved, and their young son Alex, along with another of my daughter's toddler friends (the dad a musician, both he and the mom speed freaks) completed the kiddie ensemble. And at the epicenter, always, was Hibiscus, running around with theatrical directions, doing his own amazing makeup, donning extraordinary headdresses, enchanting the likes of audiences that included Allen Ginsberg, Stevie Wonder and uptown socialites.

I remember serving Hibiscus quasi-macrobiotic meals in my Brooklyn apartment, with enormous joints for dessert. Jack was almost always with Hibiscus, but despite his efforts, in the shadow of his charisma. Hibiscus could truly act, sing and dance and his beauty was breathtaking. At twenty-two years old, I didn't appreciate the cultural revolutionary that Hibiscus truly was. Bridging drag queen kitsch with egalitarian ethos, he truly embodied radical fairy philosophy and gay liberation, long before the term was hatched.

I remember going to Stevie Wonder's midtown New Year's Eve party. Me, dressed by the Angels of Light in a thirties thrift store gown with so much makeup I didn't recognize myself. My daughter also came, beautifully made up and attired in retro attire, but no match for the little black kids wrapped in fur.

Enormous amounts of cocaine and champagne, fancy uptown guests mingling with the Angels. Hibiscus was habitually broke, which didn't bother him too much. He truly embraced the prevalent hippie philosophy and led a blatantly hedonistic lifestyle, with the charm of an all American boy turned woodland sprite. He was a natural leader, a creative spirit that allowed a motley crew of young people to transmute to performers living their wildest fantasies.

I remember Hibiscus's distinctive handwriting – an artistic calligraphy. Somehow, as my marriage ended, Rumi Missabu came to live with me, as roommate, nanny, mentor. He taught me to bake bread. Then I think Hibiscus went off to Europe, or maybe returned to California. I don't remember any official goodbyes. In those days, friends and lovers drifted in and out of our lives. I moved to the country.

On rare trips back to my hometown, I ran into Marsha [P. Johnson], who looked worse for the wear, or Rollerena, a roller skating audience member. Or black leather garbed Matt, who still lived on Christopher Street. I saw some ads for Hibiscus and his sisters, performing in downtown venues. I heard Hibiscus had cut his hair, maybe was working in a soap opera. And then I saw his memorial poster at Sheridan Square and he became my first friend to die from "gay cancer."

How lucky we were to be young in such an enchanted, and more innocent time. Hibiscus brought magic and mayhem with him, and how fortunate was my toddler daughter to be exposed to such explosive and communal creativity. Hibiscus epitomized love and liberation. Those of us who knew him, or saw his performances were truly blessed.

The East Coast Angels of Light shows were always magical, musical and gender-bending extravaganzas drenched in glitter against a backdrop of the political malaise of the 1970s. Photo: Sheyla Baykal, The Angels of Light, Theater for the New City, NYC, 1972

History tells us that being gay has been fraught with hostility, aggression, terror and self-oppression in order to survive in any given social paradigm. Gay rights have been evolving slowly throughout American history. Gay tolerance has been and is a whole other uphill battle. Even in the beginning of the 21st Century, the LGBTQ community continues to struggle with political freedoms, social acceptance, equality and human rights. In many countries there are harsh punishments, including death, to those who openly choose a same-sex lifestyle. (7)

Unlike many of the beautiful people who passed through the Angels of Light, Hibiscus was lucky; he wasn't hassled often by the cops. He never tried to hide as a gay man. He insisted on shining his brightest light and bringing attention to his life style that offended certain parts of society. Although he could blend in because of his all-American appearance, Hibiscus faced his share of intolerance. "Freak," "Fag" and "Weirdo" were slurs hurled his way, which often were answered with an angry reaction from Angel Jack, who defended George with his fists.

Photo top: Sheyla Baykal, The Angels of Light, Theater for the New City, NYC, 1973; bottom: Portrait by Charles Caron, NYC, 1973

Tim Robbins

I have often reflected on those days as an important and woefully unknown moment in time that I was fortunate enough to witness. The Angels of Light were way ahead of their time. These were liberated and free souls putting it out there for all to see, in a gloriously camp way before it was fashionable and, more importantly, before it was safe to do so. I remember their courage and their outrageous pride in who they were and how it contrasted with the rigid homophobic neighborhood swells in the Village at that time. (8)

Andrew Sherwood
Photographer and family friend
(Photo circa 1985)

I saw him for the first time in New York
City, crossing Astor Place and holding
hands with a beautiful girl while limping.
A thunderbolt struck me and I spoke of
them to my friends for months. To my
amazement, I found them at a rehearsal,
where the little girl, his sister Jayne Anne,
was playing the role of Christopher Robin in a delightful
musical, *Sing Ho For a Bear.* His entire family was present,
eagerly watching the actors while growling at Jayne Anne if she
was not perfect. We bonded that day, in the Mecca of avant-
garde dance and theater that was Judson Memorial Church at
that time.

What an amazing family: father, mother, three boys and three
girls, all crazy about theater and resolved to conquer New York.
At the age of eight, George III had led the family on stage,
forcing his father to leave an insurance job, his mother from her
female role in the home, his siblings from their childish games
and the Florida home (they abandoned it furnished) to live,
eight-as-one in a New York slum, where they slept on the floor
wrapped in quilts against the cold, to live their mad dream. He
was only fifteen when we met.

George sketched imported dresses and old-fashioned shoes,
"Shoes by Seville," worn by fashionable women who talked in
cartoon bubbles to say one word: "Hot!" He accompanied his
siblings to auditions that required songs, for Broadway, Off and
Off-Off, for commercials, fashion and modeling, and he
watched them until the end. They were seen everywhere, and
soon the whole family was the talk of New York.

George became Hibiscus at San Francisco after being a slave of
love in an organic farm where he learned to print poems that he

distributed on the street corners. In 1972, during a visit to the US, I was called upon by the Harris family to play in their new show, *Gossamer Wings*, which was ready to open at Theater for the New City. After much hesitation, I let myself be won by old memories and, of course, a healthy dose of curiosity. I had not seen George since he left for San Francisco in 1966. Now Hibiscus, the strange boy director was covered with sumptuous fabrics and hurled into the air handfuls of glitter exclaiming, "It's so beautiful!" Still crazy, I told myself.

Gossamer Wings opened. If I told you the room was celebrating the creation of the world, that would be too simple because, alongside Adam and Eve, we saw Carmen and her gypsy, Pandora and her box, with all the evil fairies who escape into it; Isadora Duncan, the earthquake in San Francisco in 1906, a patriotic tap dance of the First World War, the grieving fiancée of a soldier killed in Vietnam singing an air of *Les Chercheuses D'or 1933*, a water ballet, a duo Skins-Rouges lover, a Krishna-baby down from his pedestal to dredge Mother Nature rowing with her children in danger, an exotic fish show, a descent into Hell, Satan's dance band, a choir of angels taking good children to heaven in the sky, clouds, thunder, lightning and primitive cells, Jupiter and Neptune, a French cancan danced by Apollo and his frenzied following—have I forgotten anything?

The audience was as ornamental and funky as the troupe. After the curtain, the famous Rollerina crossed the room on roller skates, dressed in a crinoline dress, wearing a fur sleeve, a taffeta hat, fishnet on hair, velvet cape, goggles, sounding a copper horn while spinning. The actors threw apples, bananas and grapes that the spectators, if they did not eat them on the spot, tossed back on stage. Actors and audience called out to one another, cheerfully heckling Rollerina with "Bitchy girl! Whore!!" and the curtain fell again. No one wanted to leave. Drunk, hovering, a little crazy, we felt at home.

Chapter 7
Meanwhile...Backstage...
The Fairy Tale...
and the end of an era

The Angels of Light singing 'Fourteen Angels' from the Engelbert Humperdinck Opera, while taking the children to heaven. Theater for the New City, NYC. Photo by Andrew Sherwood, circa 1973

By the mid-1970s, what was going on behind the scenes was often more dramatic than what was happening onstage. Grim realities of survival, changing cultural values and the rising cost of living were settling dangerously close to Hibiscus' and Angel Jack's lives. Their "new normal" manifested as dried up funding for shows and the loss of their most reliable patrons due to death, loss of wealth and/or changing ideas about how art should be delivered to the public. This darkening paradigm was terrorizing artists across an array of genres.

Hibiscus and Jack had hard choices to make—whether to tone down their extravaganzas or engage in unscrupulous ways of bringing in funds, as did many of their friends. Talk of turning tricks (exchanging sex for money) filled the air.

"The trucks" were a New York City stomping ground for gay trysts. These assignations satisfied thrill-seekers' cravings for sex, money, danger and adventure. Hibiscus' sisters remember him bringing them along to the notorious trucks when there were no babysitters on hand. While waiting for him and Angel Jack to complete their transactions in this intensely frightening and potentially dangerous environment, his sisters distracted themselves by reading whatever was written on the trucks. They were surprised to see show posters amongst the graffiti.

New York was intensely dirty and gritty in those days. For the LGBTQ community, New York was an impossible scenario as far as choices of lifestyle, livelihood and survival. The Angels of Light troupe was filled with wonderful men, women and transgender folk who were denied typical opportunities for employment, schooling and creating families of their own. Sometimes, their only options for survival were sex work and living on the fringes of society where they would be less safe, but at least could earn enough to keep a roof over their heads.

Rival troupes and artists competed with each other for attention with panache (and bitchiness). Troupes like Larry Ray's Trockedero De Monte Carlo, Charles Ludlam's Theater of the Ridiculous, Jackie Curtis' Hot Peaches, and individual artists including Charles Busch, Candy Darling and Holly Woodlawn had subtly or overtly antagonistic relationships with Hibiscus and the Angels of Light. In hindsight, this rivalry kept all of them moving forward and evolving artistically, which eventually led to their importance in the counter-culture and created a legitimacy and admiration of their art within mainstream society. This credence was a necessary beacon of light that shone clearly on LGBTQ issues in order to gain tolerance so that human rights and new laws could be considered.

138

Other issues for Hibiscus' budding teenage sisters to sort out were Women's Liberation and skewed sexual and mating modeling from their cast-mates and artistic peers. Their wonder years played out in this potently charged, gender-bending environment.

Jayne Anne, Eloise and Mary Lou Harris were "straight" by nature, but socialized as gay men. This radical layering was genuine, a recipe for a rich life indeed, both for themselves and their future families. One of Hibiscus' sisters lost her virginity to a gorgeous gay boy in Berlin, an Angels of Light cast member, who later became a beautiful transgender woman in The Romy Haag Drag Troupe.

Aside from typical sibling rivalry, an early love-hate relationship developed between George and his sisters. Although he paid them much attention, he would abscond with their dolls to change their sex. An early demonstration of gender bending, no doubt. George would shower one sister with starring roles and glamorous costumes and jewelry, as a gambit to get the other sisters to work harder for their place in the spotlight. This would almost always lead to brutal arguments between the girls, while George happily skipped off to see what other family mischief he could instigate.

(1)

George ingratiated his mother to the point of her being too distracted to notice that her daughters needed emotional protection from him.

In Georgia O' Keeffe's *Golden Hibiscus* painting, the flower dominates the canvas, leaving little room for foliage and other growth in the environment. Let's just say that this is also true when it came to Hibiscus and his sisters. Exacerbating the chaos surrounding them was the ever-present danger of unwittingly ingesting tabs of LSD or angel dust-laced foods at the never-ending parade of parties, opening night soirees with other theatrical troupes, hippie gatherings and plain old everyday life in the party-hardy, artsy bohemianism of the era.

In 1974, The Angels of Light opened for the film premiere of Ladies and Gentlemen, The Rolling Stones *at New York's Ziegfeld Theater. Hibiscus, who had spent his career until now fighting for free theater, shockingly accepted pay for his troupe to perform a vignette before the film – dancing up and down the aisles and throwing frisbees to the audience. This photo, taken by a photographer for the New York Daily News, demonstrates that the shows were becoming work rather than being magical. Hibiscus and his Angels had hit a wall – they needed something new. (Photo: New York Daily News) (2)*

Robert Heide

Now the 70's transitioned into a decade of sex for the sake of sex as in the days of the Weimar Republic in early 1930s Germany. On Christopher Street in the Village, then called the cruisiest street in town, sex began to take place in doorways and in the trucks at night down on West Street on the river. The new gay fashions that were all the rage had men standing around wearing lumberjack shirts open to the navel and tight fitting torn dungarees. Andy Warhol and his Silver Factory entourage were in evidence in a special VIP room at Studio 54. Another 'in-crowd' gathering place was the Continental Baths, which was in the basement of the Ansonia Hotel on the upper West Side. It advertised itself to its gay clientele as "The Glory of Ancient Rome." Entertainment was the order of the day (and night) and it is the place where the Divine Miss M – Bette Midler – first did her vocalizing with Barry Manilow pounding the ivories alongside the swimming pool.

Serendipity drew timely miracles to Hibiscus. Right after the *Ladies and Gentlemen, The Rolling Stones* premiere, Hibiscus and Angel Jack received a letter from a film company in Belgium that was shooting a film with Maurice Bejart, the Swiss choreographer. Bejart wanted George and Jack to come to Belgium and appear in fantasy scenes.

François Weyergans
Belgian writer, director, and filmmaker.
Excerpt from a letter to Hibiscus and Angel Jack, 1974:

Maurice Bejart talked to me about your wonderful play. He was very excited by your work. The film is a story based on the characters of some of Maurice's ballets. The film is the story of a man who questions others in order to find himself. He wanders in the mountains, delirious. Two men (you) dressed in spangled robes, wearing mitres, offer him a bicycle and accompany him, pushing the bicycle.

Could you read in the Holy Bible, in Zachariah, chapter 4, 5 and 6: perhaps we can arrange something in the same spirit (same mind)?

Moonbeams too…
François Weyergans (3)

Above and below: Hibiscus and Angel Jack in Belgium for the Bejart film

While filming in Belgium, they met Ritsaert ten Cate, artistic director of the Mickery Theater in Amsterdam and a National Artist of Holland. He was enchanted by Hibiscus and Angel Jack's energy and visual aesthetic. Like a prince in a fairy tale, Ritsaert invited the entire cast of the Angels of Light to perform at the Mickery Theater and arranged a sponsored European tour. This gave Hibiscus and the Angels an enormous vote of confidence.

Governments across Europe appreciated the arts and subsidized many American theater troupes in order to bring their theatrical and political ideas to their countries. With full support from the government of The Netherlands, Ritsaert leveraged his status and resources to support emerging artists on the scene.

With grant money supplied by Ritsaert and the Mickery, a euphoric Hibiscus and Angel Jack returned to New York from Belgium and immediately rented a huge house in Tannersville to begin writing, casting, rehearsing, and building sets and costumes for a new European tour extravaganza, to be called *Razzamatazz*. The house had been a hotel with 18 bedrooms and a red British-style telephone booth on the first floor.

Angels of Light 1975 European tour. Photo taken at the Mickery Theater in Amsterdam. Photo: Harris family archives

One by one, cast members began to arrive in the sleepy little village of Tannersville in the Catskill Mountains. The New York Trailways bus brought daily thespian delights in full make-up, costumes, drag, hair and headdresses. The streets of Tannersville became decorated with glitter, sequins and beads. Rumi Missabu, David Loehr, Chuck Dancer, Java Jet (now Bambi Lake) and Miss Marsha sauntered down the country roads and Main Street, singing show tunes and creating a peaceful parade of townspeople who were curious and maybe a little frightened, who sometimes followed them to Hibiscus' house. Tannersville had never been exposed to such a spectacle. However, with the towns of Woodstock and Bethel for neighbors, they were used to hippies, so thankfully no confrontations occurred. It helped that David Loehr took a job in town to help pay the rent and show the locals a friendly face.

Friends and loyal financial backers Robin Archer-Moles and Frederick Combs (an actor from *The Boys in the Band)*, arranged for Hibiscus

143

and the Angels to prepare for the European tour by previewing the shows at the Provincetown Playhouse on Cape Cod. The cast stayed at the Owl's Nest Hotel in "P-town" and staged a pre-show street parade up the main drag to the theater every night. It was a 1974 end-of-summer celebration that went on for a week. The Angels of Light were treated to disco dancing at the A-House nightclub and to fabulous beach jaunts every day. The sand dunes were enormous. Provincetown set the mood for the Angels of Light like no other place could.

Ritsaert's vision was that Hibiscus and the Angels of Light would create a rainbow lens through which people could experience a world where acceptance of being gay was possible. He scheduled a tour that included the Mickery Theater in Amsterdam; Academie Der Kunst in Berlin; the Nancy Festival in Nancy, France; and Le Campaign Premiere Theatre in Paris.

Ritsaert encouraged Hibiscus and the Angels to freely explore the furthest frontiers of their creativity. In their artistry he recognized a panacea for the social and political

Ritsaert ten Cate, Mickery Theatre, Amsterdam Holland, 1975

woes of the times. The Angels of Light opened *Razzmatazz,* a glittering extravaganza, in 1975 at The Mickery Theater in Amsterdam. The cast included Hibiscus, Ann, and siblings Fred, Jayne Anne, Eloise and Mary Lou. Cast members from San Francisco and New York included Java Jet, John Rothermel and Chuck Dancer. European cast members included Chandra and Mr. Greece 1975.

144

L to R: Mary Lou, Jayne Anne and Eloise in Europe, 1975.
Harris family archives

Amsterdam was a delightful playground for the cast. They performed eight shows a week and then headed down to the Leidseplein (à la Times Square in NYC), Melkweg and the "red light" district to score blocks of hashish and look at the fabulous girls in the windows to get ideas from their erotic fashions. Happy and stoned, the Angels of Light rode bikes to Vondelpark Park by day and played all night in dance clubs and pubs, even though some in the cast were sorely underage. Billows of hashish smoke poured from their hotel windows, and they seemed to float above the ground through the Amsterdam portion of their tour. Ritsaert was extremely caring when it came to Hibiscus' sisters. He often gave them extra money to buy food at local restaurants and twice arranged for them to stay, safely, at his assistant Yvonne's apartment. Years later, Ritsaert reunited with Ann, Eloise and Mary Lou at La MaMa's art gallery in Manhattan. He seemed surprised, and *very* relieved, to see the sisters grown up and thriving, and was thrilled to meet Eloise's infant daughter, Montana. He gave them a big hug and said, "I was always worried about you, but you were tough little girls who seemed to know instinctively how to stay safe in such an extreme theatrical environment."

Harris family friend **Agosto Machado**, performer and activist, was touring in Amsterdam at the time with Ellen Stewart's La MaMa Troupe. He remembers following a trail of glitter from the Mickery Theater to a small hotel on Frans van Mierisstraat. Realizing that Hibiscus and the Angels of Light must be in town pleased this dear family friend.

Agosto Machado at Veselka Diner, East Village, NYC, 2015

After a successful run at the Mickery in Amsterdam, The Angels of Light were invited by Mike Figgis of The Peoples Theatre troupe in London to participate in his show called *The Boston Concept.* The show required three small stages to be positioned around the theater space. The audience was moved between them in giant boxes with bleachers for seats that floated on compressed air as technicians moved them around. The audience had to come back on three consecutive nights to experience the entire show and the Angels of Light cast members had to be in different parts of the room for different scenes. The grand finale of the show, for the entire audience to see, was The Angels of Light doing the military tap to "You're a Grand Old Flag" accompanied by a military band with Hibiscus as the Grand Marshall bandleader. Behind them were images projected onto a screen of President Nixon from the beginning of his career to his spectacular downfall, each image looking more menacing than the previous one. (Mike later was nominated for two Academy Awards for writing and directing the critically acclaimed film *Leaving Las Vegas*).

For all this, unbeknownst to Hibiscus, Europe for him and for the Angels would prove both a fairy tale and the end of an era. A glaring oversight occurred in the programming of the tour after the Angels' initial month in Amsterdam. They had a six-week hiatus between Amsterdam and their next performance in France. The cast was in

A panic as no one had money or a place to live. Mike Figgis offered to take several cast members, including Ann and Fred, back to London to live on his artist's compound. Hibiscus, Angel Jack, Mr. Greece, Mary Lou, and Eloise would live on Mykonos in Greece for the hiatus. Jayne Anne returned to New York and the European cast members found friends and family in nearby countries that could house them temporarily. It was a cliffhanging six weeks. The sightseeing was magnificent, but no one had money to eat.

The Londoners survived on bread, fish and ale. Hibiscus and Angel Jack abandoned Mary Lou and Eloise the minute they hit Mykonos. The girls, barely into their teens, realized they had been left vulnerable and exposed. So they improvised. They found jobs dancing with tourists at a popular dance club. They earned just enough for two meals a day and a nice room with running water in a safe hotel. Their

youth, dancing skills and ability to speak English was a big plus with the tourists. Meanwhile, while Hibiscus and Angel Jack thrived on Mykonos, doing shows on the beach with Mr. Greece and living like kings, Mary Lou and Eloise came to the alarming realization that they were invited to Greece only so they could smuggle hashish in their underwear – because if *they* got arrested, they would simply be deported, whereas George and Jack would have gone to a Greek prison for a long time. This painful breach of trust cut to the heart, and made the girls wary of their brother for a long time after.

Mr. Greece on the beach in Mykonos with Hibiscus and Angel Jack. Photo by Do Lee, 1975

Six weeks later the hungry hiatus was finally over. The Angels of Light received their tour money and tickets to travel and were presented at the Festival Mondial du Théâtre in Nancy, France.

The Angels were housed in an elegant modern flat, replete with the record albums of Barbara Streisand, The Supremes, Judy Garland and Al Jolson singing "Swanee." With all of the elegant treatment that the Angels received in France, they forgot about the political tensions of the world, which were reflected by a variety of theater troupes at the Nancy Festival. Instead, the Angels of Light's musicals celebrated peace, love, humanity, unfettered self-expression and sunshine. Audiences loved it.

After Nancy they were off to Berlin. As their bus drove through the wall to East Berlin, somber conversations couldn't help but color the mood. The bus was pulled over and border guards came on board, asking questions. The cast looked bizarre with their shaved eyebrows and gender-imaginative apparel. They were terrified because they had hidden large hunks of hashish in the tires and interior panels of the bus. A quick-thinking theater manager explained that the Angels of Light were government-sponsored artists, en route to the Akademie Der Kunst to perform at an International Conference of Cultural Affairs. The skeptical guards were satisfied and let them continue on their way. It was the closest Hibiscus and his Angels had ever come to being in real trouble with the law—and in a foreign country no less.

Jack Lang, the Nancy Festival creator and later France's minister of culture, organized a photo opportunity on the steps of Nancy's Grand Hotel for politician and future president of France, François Mitterrand, to 'glitter' with the Angels of Light, circa 1975.

Angel Jack had become the enforcer, the guy who made Hibiscus' wishes, whims, ideas and mania come to life and sometimes not in the most pleasant of ways. Jack wore many hats in Hibiscus' world – lover, set designer, negotiator, protector and strict and often mean-spirited taskmaster. That said, Hibiscus was used to having that kind of presence in his life. His mother, albeit unknowingly, was the original enforcer through her undying devotion to his ideas, lifestyle and personality. Ann thrived on being the enchanted participant in the fairytale life that Hibiscus was providing her.

As a teenager, Ann had endured harsh realities when, in a steady progression, members of her immediate family died – her father in a car accident on the way home from a dentist convention, driving overnight to make it in time for his son's baseball game; her brother from a devastating muscular disease; and her mother soon after from uterine cancer. Her grandfather, Jim Driscoll, with whom she was particularly close, died on the very day Ann carried the flag to lead the Fourth of July Parade. This honor had been a long-held dream of hers as a Girl Scout. When she came home to find her beloved grandpa gone, it reinforced a recurring pattern in her young life that led her to believe that for every good thing that happened to her, an equally devastating one would follow.

Left to survive with her aunt, Ann vowed early on that a life filled with fantasy and enchantment was her heart's desire. And she never steered away from that direction. Having Hibiscus as her first born was like hitting the fantasy lottery!

Angel Jack was beginning to show signs of aggression and resentment toward Hibiscus and his family. He teased the girls constantly. Any time a female came out of a bathroom, Jack would say that they smelled. "Whew ... honey, change that rag!" Earlier in the tour, Jack viciously accused Ann of being "old," often right before her cue to go onstage. She was only forty-nine and could tap dance circles around any member of the cast. Hibiscus began to take serious note of Jack's antagonism toward his family.

Ann Harris as a comet. The Angels of Light, Mickery Theatre, Amsterdam 1975

In earlier years, Angel Jack would remember birthdays and make special costumes for the family when he was feeling extra loving. Initially, he took non-singing roles in the shows because he could not carry a tune or dance, but quickly found his vocal footing after hearing Eartha Kitt and modeled his husky voice after hers. He was in fact a wonderful design artist and produced sets and costumes that were both magical and clunky. He was never afraid to try out an idea.

Angel Jack

> The shows gave me something to *do*. George kept everything *moving* – a crazy-ass kaleidoscope of people and projects. He could draw things out of me, hidden talents. His genius was his way of bringing people together and his instinct for who was right for what task. George learned that nagging was the best way to motivate me. "I need 10 unicorns BY TONIGHT!!" I made everything to impress him. He knew I was the best, but wouldn't ever tell me.

Do Lee

> I found some paying work in New York, and other places to stay, and did not go with the Angels of Light to the Holland Festival. But I did get a call from Paris to come and help backstage, and a ticket—which turned out to be one way! The piano player was the first to quit (he was, I think, a friend of Chandra's and on a high horse that he had been in the band

Cockney Rebel) and then the AV technician. So I ran the light board, as well as managing sets and costumes.

Hibiscus did his best to drum up publicity and a VIP audience for the show. He and Angel Jack went for an audition at the Moulin Rouge, which made the Holland Festival theater owner furious – so he closed down the show and locked the doors while the people were standing in line outside waiting to come in.

The press was very kind to The Angels of Light during their European tour, showering them everywhere with validating praise.

Last stop: Paris. Hibiscus' *Les Angels de Lumiere* at Le Campaign Premiere Theatre was the big tour finale. Due to dwindling funds, most of the cast members were told to go home, including Ann, Fred, Eloise and Mary Lou.

After, Hibiscus wrote to his mother who would act as a communications director in order to help him problem solve or to send songs, money and human resources.

Dear Mom,

<u>S.O.S.</u> We have been offered to play the Swiss Festival (remember we met them in Nancy) starting Sept. 18. Only quick action (or a miracle) can make it work. <u>Please Please</u> send tape of music and Photostats as soon as possible. We will most likely have to use the tape as background so be sure to include all chorus of each song. <u>Please don't forget,</u> As for a cast that's another miracle to perform. Right now there's only two of us. I'm not counting at all on Johnny and Chuck – you know how they are, and I heard they are taking hormones in Berlin. Ick! So we are searching in town for talent. But how to rehearse them with no music? Wish you were here!

We have to meet Koko on Sept. 9 to see a theatre she has lined up. The people who are backing the show in Paris think it's very important for you & the girls to be in the show, but are not willing to put up the money for plane tickets. But the television people (remember we spoke of this) want Mary Lou anyway for a T.V. special and will send for her for this, and for the show. So I was thinking, why not combine Weezy's and her role into one (please keep this secret), and have her star in the London and Paris shows. Then she can return with us before Christmas after the London show. Koko (who is a professor) has offered to tutor her – and Jack Lang and his wife have offered for Lou to stay with them and his daughter in Paris.

Is there any solution that could make this possible? Who else could possibly play the lead? If she has a tutor isn't it possible she could leave school until December? Please think about it.

Please remember, <u>S.O.S.</u> on tapes and photostat music. Hope all is well. Did Walter come? I hope so. Please send me his address – I only have his old one.

Love to All
G III

Fourteen-year-old Mary Lou did return from New York, flying to Paris to perform in *Les Angels de Lumiere* at Le Campaign Premiere Theatre. The cast settled into an apartment in the Montparnasse district of Paris. They performed eight shows a week to very colorful audiences and lived a free and elegant lifestyle – shopping on the Champs-Élysées and sitting in French cafes for hours soaking in their new glamorous world.

During the run of the Paris show an eccentric executive from the Mazda Light Company hired Hibiscus and his troupe to perform specialized concerts for corporate shows. The money they made from these shows turbo-charged their lifestyles. The cast was given a large apartment in a beautiful section of Paris. They were squired around town in private cars and invited to the chicest events.

Hibiscus' youngest sister Mary Lou, in Paris, 1975

After four months, the spell was broken. The Mazda Light Company abruptly stopped showering the Angels with cars, gifts and performance opportunities. They were told to vacate the apartment in two weeks. One by one, cast members reluctantly returned home.

George, Walter Michael and Fred dropped out of high school in order to accept professional advancement opportunities that were too good to pass up, as when Walter Michael was cast in the original Broadway production of *HAIR*. Before Hibiscus and Angel Jack came back on the scene, balancing theater and school was barely manageable for the Harris sisters. With the Europe tour it became impossible. Jayne Anne, now in high school, was old enough to drop out if she needed to – but for Eloise and Mary Lou, now in junior high school, respectively, leaving school altogether was legally out of the question. Dealing with truancy became a new dynamic in their lives because of the Angels' grueling rehearsal and performance schedules.

After several years of the girls' schooling getting in the way of their shows, Hibiscus and Angel Jack thought it would be a good idea if Mary Lou married Angel Jack, acquire adult legal status, and bypass the truancy issue. As gung-ho as Ann Harris was to solve all of George's problems, this idea was too far beyond the pale.

The Paris cast included Hibiscus, Angel Jack, Mary Lou (bottom left), Chandra, John Rothermel (bottom right) and several French dancers.
Photo: Paris, France 1975

Dear Mom,   Paris, France 1975

How are you? Sorry it's been so long since I've written but
things have been so busy here it's impossible to find time to
write. First let me tell you I'm very impressed by the songs you
wrote for the new show, they sound really great.

Lots is happening here. Let me start from the beginning. This
theatre is the pits. Nothing they promised has come through
and Koko is looking for another theater to open in. They have
broken the contract right down the line.

1) The publicity promised has not come through. All newspaper,
   etc. has come through our contacts in Nancy.
2) He's <u>completely</u> cheating us financially and Koko has lawyers
   in to try and straighten out the contract.
3) He cheated us on the T.V. deal and lawyers are trying to clear
   this up.

Although many celebrities have come and seen the show and
many important people have come by word of mouth, it's the
"<u>in</u>" cult show in Paris and we have a big following. It's a
shame we ran into another Lucille-type theater manager. We do
have the Mazda Lighting contract and David Hockney, the
Rothschilds, Koko & Jack Lang are looking for a new theatre
to open Dec. 1. After we close here Nov. 15 we open in
Brussels for a week. Although we are being cheated here we
have nice apartments and 3 good meals a day in the restaurant.
Lou is fine and I take good care of her. Although Java is on the
poster (wishful thinking), he's not here. Will try to work on
more tickets for you, Jane and Weezy [Eloise].

Problem #2
We have to do something about Lou's school situation. After
talking with the lawyers etc. we have a solution, it may sound
sudden but it's the best way. Please think seriously about it –
for Lou to marry Jack with parents consent here at the
American Embassy. She instantly is adult status and can get
working papers and be free of the school problem. What do

you think? Koko and the lawyers think it's the best idea – then Lou and Jack could always get an annulment. It's only the papers of marriage that are needed. Will send you further details.

Other than the bad news of the theatre manager, Paris has been very good to us. We are taken out in Rolls Royces to chi-chi clubs and are having a good time. Your pay for songs is part of the legal suit with Jean Bougein.

Love, G III

Never ones to panic about suddenly being homeless, hungry or out-of-luck due to the sudden loss of the Paris show and accommodations, Hibiscus and Angel Jack booked a show somewhere on the Ivory Coast of Africa. While they fulfilled one last engagement in Paris, they wanted Mary Lou to fly to Africa ahead of them, but at 15 she was uncomfortable going there alone. She decided to return home instead.

On New Year's morning of 1976, Mary Lou secretly packed. Once again she thanked God and her mother for the advice of always keeping enough money for a taxi to the airport and to hide her return trip airline ticket from Jack and Hibiscus. As she was sneaking out of the apartment in the early morning hours, an angry Angel Jack jumped in front of her with a demonic look on his face. He said, "Where are you going?" Mary Lou said, "I want to go home!" Angel Jack became agitated and seized her suitcase. Hibiscus appeared, grabbed Jack's arm and pulled him away. "Let her go, Jackie!" Jack punched him while screaming, "She *has* to go to Africa, you idiot." Mary Lou was terrified. Hibiscus jumped on Angel Jack, held him down, and told his sister to "RUN!"

Shaking uncontrollably, Mary Lou ran as fast as she could, jumped in a cab and sped off to Charles De Gaulle airport, sobbing the entire way. She knew that George had probably taken a bad beating. Jack was furious. But Mary Lou knew Hibiscus was relieved knowing that he had saved her from an experience that could have turned out badly.

156

Soon after, Hibiscus and The Angels of Light found themselves back in New York City disoriented and without a theatrical home, funds, or a place to sleep. After performing in Europe for three years, it was as if New York had forgotten them. Or worse, didn't need them anymore.

Hibiscus and his increasingly quarrelsome lover lived with the Harris family in their tight-quartered East Village apartment in Manhattan for the time being. Angel Jack's mother, Bette Coe, gave the boys enough money to eat for a few weeks.

Mary Lou (center) between Jack and George in Paris, 1975. From Harris family archives

By this time the youthful hippie ideals of peace, love, freedom and happiness were hurriedly fading away. The youth culture was moving away from communal freedoms and towards the capitalistic self-interest of individuals. The 1980s were fast approaching.

Paris, then, became the true end of a glorious, creative, glittering and free-spirited fairy tale for The Angels of Light...the death rattle was about to begin.

Chapter 8
The Shocking Pink Life of Jayne Champagne

From Award Winning European Tour
HIBISCUS AND ANGEL JACK
PRESENT

FEMME FATALE

THE SHOCKING PINK LIFE OF JAYNE CHAMPAGNE
Featuring
HIBISCUS , ANGEL JACK, JAVA, SUGAR, MR. GREECE, ELOISE, CHI CHI

MONTGOMERY PLAYHOUSE
622 BROADWAY (at Grant Ave.)

OPENS AUGUST 5, 1976 AT 8-30 P.M.
TICKETS (415) 788-8282 $5.00 GENERAL ADMISSION
SPECIAL MIDNIGHT SHOWS FRIDAY and SATURDAY
ORIGINAL MUSIC by ANN HARRIS

Hibiscus and Angel Jack were broke and running out of luck. They had to come up with creative styles of making money. Jack made a valiant attempt at bartending, which he vehemently hated. But Hibiscus was street savvy and knew how to survive. Faced with what seemed like inescapable or problematic circumstances, he contacted George Cory, his friend and one-time benefactor, and begged him to sponsor The Angels of Lights' BIG return to San Francisco. Begging was a first for Hibiscus and he hated it.

George Cory, who had written the music for the hit song "I Left My Heart in San Francisco," made famous by Tony Bennett, agreed to sponsor Hibiscus' new show, *Femme Fatale: The Shocking Pink Life of Jayne Champagne,* at The Montgomery Playhouse in San Francisco. The cast included Hibiscus as Jayne Champagne, Angel Jack, Eloise, Java Jet (Bambi Lake), Sugar, Mr. Greece and San Francisco's dancer extraordinaire, Chi Chi.

Hibiscus as Jayne Champagne.
Photo by Dan Nicoletta, circa 1977

Cory supplied Hibiscus with a 1959 Jaguar with an exotic hardwood interior and an apartment in San Francisco's Mission District. The show was based on the life of actress Jayne Mansfield and her muscle-builder husband, Mickey Hargitay. It was the perfect subject for Hibiscus and Angel Jack, as their own relationship was growing tumultuous.

The East Coast Angels of Light had not yet performed in their founder's old stomping grounds. Knowing he would be under intense scrutiny, it was important to Hibiscus that his return to San Francisco be a home run, a sold-out show that would be the height of fabulousness. He was eager to start rehearsing.

Angel Jack devised trippy geometric-shaped headdresses and cascading Las Vegas type showgirl costumes. *Femme Fatale: The Shocking Pink Life of Jayne Champagne* pulled out all the stops. The press swarmed the highly anticipated opening. During the run, Hibiscus invited the San Francisco chapter of the Holy Order of MANS to the show. This was the new age monastery that Walter Michael, had joined in the late 1960s. Whenever Hibiscus visited his

159

brother there, he was paranoid that the holy brothers and sisters could read his mind – and so, perversely, he thought the naughtiest thoughts he could muster. With Walter Michael now living in far away Detroit, Hibiscus enlisted Eloise to invite his brother's colleagues to the show. When they demurred, Eloise leapt into high gear and challenged them to a debate, using their own religious philosophy to convince them to attend. It was a triumph for Hibiscus when they turned up in the front row of the theater, wearing their clerical garb. Hibiscus directed an especially naughty performance at their pious minds. Back in Detroit, Walter Michael heard that they really enjoyed the show.

The show looked beautiful but was sullied by Hibiscus and Angel Jack's constant arguing. Although still together, their tension and schism would grow bigger as time went on. Cast members would walk into the theater to be met by chocolate donuts being hurled at them by an angry and hostile Angel Jack who was fuming about a multitude of subjects, as his relationship with Hibiscus began to unravel. Photo by Dan Nicoletta, circa 1976

Hibiscus and Angel Jack were lovers, competitors, best friends and enemies all wrapped into one big glitter ball. Jack was methodical and critical – Hibiscus was free spirited and visionary. George would have a creative impulse and, like magic, the universe and its foot soldiers began to spin his wishes to life with Hibiscus as its glorious center.

160

Jack, on the other hand, had to work extra hard (or throw a tantrum) to get his ideas taken seriously. He was truly inspired and creative when designing and executing sets and costumes. But Jack was tone deaf, couldn't sing very well, and labored in Hibiscus' shadow, cast as the Devil or some other aggressive character in the shows. Eventually Jack's characters took hold of him and amplified his true nature.

Dan Nicoletta
Photographer, author

More Glitter – Less Bitter

I was in Los Angeles in November 2008 photographing a demonstration against Proposition 8, the California ballot initiative that repealed same sex marriage legal protections in the State. In the crowd was a lad with a hand made placard encrusted in glitter that read "More Glitter - Less Bitter." His slogan immediately became one of my favorite mantras in life, but Hibiscus and The Angels of Light theatre group had planted

Dan Nicoletta, photo by Amron

the seeds of that delightful notion within me, long before in 1975. And though Hibiscus didn't live to see same-sex marriage approved by the US Supreme Court in 2015, how he lived his life was instrumental in fostering that cultural sea change. To many of us, the role of Hibiscus as a beacon of possibility is unequivocal....

The late Martin Worman, [co]-lyricist of the music of The Cockettes and The Angels Light, was fond of regaling me with tales of the early years of The Cockettes, which I had missed out on (they formally disbanded in 1972). It was Martin who first implied that Hibiscus, with his unique blend of spirituality and show biz élan, would be remembered as a significant force for the societal changes to come, and I couldn't agree more. Whether it's the mainstream acceptance of people and ideas outside the contemporary binary gender norms or today's drag culture capturing the imagination of most corners of the world... it is lovely to realize how prescient Hibiscus was at a time when culture did not support that very well.

I joined in the fun in 1975 with the Angels as a photographer for the group, but I was really more of a groupie... following key people in the group around like an adoring puppy dog, trying to get the definitive portrait of these ephemeral sadhu-like creatures in drag.

It was through Martin Worman that I first heard of the now famous photo with Hibiscus inserting the carnation into the pointing gun of the Military Police at the demonstration against the Vietnam War at the Pentagon in 1967... and thankfully, through David Weissman and Bill Weber's remarkable documentary film *The Cockettes* (released in 2002), that moment at the Pentagon and the man at the center of it have come to embody the intersection of the social justice movements of the 60's with the journey of the LGBT civil rights movement.

At age 20, I may not have thought about those kinds of "larger" issues... I was thinking about the next photograph I would make, how I was going to pay for that roll of film with my skimpy paycheck, who will be my next boyfriend, etc. But, I DID know to be there when Hibiscus and company rolled through town in SF in 1977 with their stage extravaganza *Femme Fatale - The Shocking Pink Life of Jane Champagne....* I knew enough to get myself over to the Montgomery Playhouse on Broadway in North Beach and plunk myself down in the front row to take pictures of these illustrious queens.... it helped that I knew Chi Chi Wilson who was one of the three cis-gendered women in the show, and who introduced me to Eloise Harris and the whole cast of characters. Everyone was very lovely and welcoming.... and they loved my photographs when I brought them back around to share. You couldn't go wrong really... there was so much Bling and talent in this show, you merely had to point and click. I also knew Larry Lara, the beautiful Latino body builder in the show, who was lovers with and the secret patron of my then-photo mentor Crawford Barton. The whole affair was very congenial... it was the first time I would meet long time photo collaborator and extraordinary chanteuse Bambi Lake, then known as Java Jet.... Bambi had worked in Berlin with the uber-famous Romy Haag Revue and you could hear a pin drop when Bambi took the stage for a solo. The presiding San Francisco Angels that I had come to know and love and work with over the previous couple of years, and who had been following a slightly different trajectory since Hibiscus had moved back to New York circa 1972, were more than slightly aghast when Hibiscus and company took SF by storm. This new show boasted to be performed by THE "original" Angels of Light and had PR that resembled more of a Las Vegas review than the multi-cultural hippie style utopian musical reviews that we had come to love and expect from the local Angels "free theatre company."

Photo by Dan Nicoletta, circa 1977

Photo of Femme Fatale *by Dan Nicoletta. Top: left to right,
Eloise Harris, Sugar, Chi Chi, Angel Jack, Bambi Lake.
Hibiscus is standing in back.*

Photo of Femme Fatale *by Dan Nicoletta. Angel Jack left,
Bambi Lake, right, circa 1977*

AND horror of horrors—this show wasn't free! The rumor that George Cory (now a reclusive elder) who originally wrote the lyrics to the Tony Bennett hit "I Left My Heart in San Francisco" was the sugar daddy for the whole affair, gave it all a particularly eccentric twist.... none-the-less we all made our way to the theatre... and many of the original Angels family and their friends were comped – in true Hibiscus egalitarian fashion... (He had, after all, split from The Cockettes over the issue keeping the shows free and he even notoriously snuck throngs of people into the full-to-capacity Cockettes shows at the Palace Theatre through sneaking them into the back door of the theater).

I went to *Femme Fatale* several times, always invited for free, and the show was always sumptuous and fun. But the show didn't last in SF. I think it ran for maybe a month or two? Perhaps the overhead of the theatre proved itself to be too high to sustain an open ended run in SF with only its provincial audiences in attendance. There were no signs of the anticipated cross over to the throngs of tourists that had been flocking to its bastard cousin playing down the block in North Beach called *Beach Blanket Babylon*. Steve Silver, the producer of that show, clearly had taken notes during his attendance at Cockette extravaganzas in the years preceding the box office gold mine that BBB had become. Finnochio's down at the other end of Broadway was a very traditional legendary drag revue, which had been running in the same club since the 1920s and which also thrived on tourist dollars... but it was huffing and puffing its last breaths. The times were strange... it was a fickle time for drag even IN the LGBT community, loyalty was not a given. Still, it WAS heady times.... and I am so grateful I got to meet and photograph these iconic and legendary performers during their hey-day...

In 1979, in NY, I reunited with Hibiscus and Eloise backstage after a Hibiscus and the Screaming Violets show and met Jayne Anne and Mary Lou for the first time.... in the wildly exuberant show Hibiscus had brilliantly modeled himself as hybrid of Liberace and a kind of big haired gay version of Elvis... I remember going backstage and greeting everyone who were still in full costume and in the complexity of the typical dysphoria/exuberance of the post show back stage world what I will never forget was that Hibiscus remembered me and addressed me by my first name.. .. it's a little thing... but it was the last time I saw him.... and so his sweetness and accessibility will forever be palpable to me....

After *Femme Fatale - The Shocking Pink Life of Jayne Champagne*, there was no denying the party was over. The era had come to an end. Hibiscus and Angel Jack fought and bickered throughout their entire time in San Francisco. They returned to New York, with no theatrical plans, nowhere to live and no money to live on.

Angel Jack demonstrated his upset and fury by taking all the sets and costumes to the Harris family's country home in the Catskills and burning them in a giant bonfire. The Angels of Light symbolically went out in a blaze of glory.

Angel Jack in the dressing room at Theater for the New City, 1979. Photo: Harris family archives

PART IV – The Finale

Hibiscus, The Cockettes and The Angels of Light had an influence in theater and in fashion as seen in the article, **Karma Chameleon** *by Horacio Silva for The New York Times (2003) (1)*

167

Chapter 9
The Gilded Cage – *Sky High*

Hibiscus, approaching 30, was experiencing a serious crisis of identity and direction. He was returning to commercial acting in New York and struggling to make steps towards maturity in his writing and career. (1979)

Hibiscus rented a beautiful garden apartment on the Upper West Side of Manhattan. He renamed himself "Brian O'Hara" for his renewed acting career in order to disassociate from George Harris III and Hibiscus. Brian O'Hara booked several television commercials and small parts on the soap operas *The Guiding Light* and *Love of Life*. His new agent, Archer King, was keeping him busy with auditions and legitimate acting work. Sugar daddies were paying the bills that acting work didn't cover.

Yearning for creative independence and beginning to feel the weight of life's financial burdens, "Brian" began to move away from Angel Jack as his lover and artistic partner. He took up with the CEO of a successful New York corporation who knew him only as Brian O'Hara. This new boyfriend cast himself in the role of protector and patron, and tried to school Brian in the benefits of financial stability.

Hibiscus and his style of art were hailed in New York, San Francisco, Paris, the Netherlands, Germany and Belgium. Success, relevance and recognition had been reached and were now firmly embedded into his psyche and his confidence. Hibiscus felt unstoppable. He became more ego-driven and his compass needle was firmly aimed toward security.

Now, with investors that he had worked tirelessly to accumulate, money was not an issue. Brian had more funding available to him than he knew what to do with.

George (right) with Colleen Whelihan-Glaser and Angel Jack, during the run of Sky High *at the Entermedia Theater, New York City, 1979.*

But the funds came with a price. The days of doing whatever he wanted, whenever he wanted, had come to a grinding halt. Brian now had businessmen, women, sugar daddies and sugar mamas to answer to. He instructed his family and friends to call him "Brian" by day and "Hibiscus" by night. His CEO boyfriend set him up in legitimate businesses including an antique store and a flower shop. Each venture was short-lived because Hibiscus never let commerce get in the way of his art. Eventually, Brian convinced his boyfriend to bankroll his new off-Broadway show, a musical called *Sky High.* This was a streamlined distillation of several Angels of Light shows. His boyfriend agreed to produce but with a high degree of control. Auditions were held.

Members of Brian's family passed muster by submitting their resumes to the CEO and were automatically cast in the show, along with other professional (unionized) actors and dancers. Gone were the opportunities to bring a creative being in to let them extend their beautiful wings and show their craft to the world. Cast members who were veteran Angels of Light lost their rights to improvise and deploy their skills in full, unfettered free expression. Songs and scenes were now pre-approved and publishing was shared with investors. Also, choreography was dictated and loyal performers who had been with Hibiscus for years had to audition for their parts.

Angel Jack was devastated. He sobbed:

> "We were friends, lovers and collaborators forever it seemed. But after he met the rich guy and decided he wanted to be a Jewish American Princess, George turned into a monster. The guy didn't know George as Hibiscus, only as 'Brian.' I had to show the guy the Angels of Light scrapbooks. Because of this heavy business influence, the new off-Broadway *Sky High* might have been done without me. I cried at the backer's audition, because I had to read for *my* Devil role!"

Promo photo, clockwise: Tommy Mathews, Angel Jack, Jayne Anne, Mary Lou, Brian O'Hara aka Hibiscus, 1979

Times were changing for Hibiscus/Brian. New York theater audiences were jaded, world-savvy and had the highest of expectations. He was consumed with worry about the audience's acceptance of his new, modernized *Sky High*. His patron's demands on the risky reconstruction of his style of theater had driven production costs through the roof.

170

Hibiscus' internal world, of Peter Pan and mythology, was in jeopardy. Now that he was charging admission, publicizing and opening in a unionized theater with union actors and wages, his new form of theater was under real grown-up scrutiny. He agonized over his expensive venture, but woefully knew that time had marched on, and that his philosophy of "free everything" was dead.

Brian was in a constant state of everything needing to be bigger – sets, costumes, musicians, performers, facilities and audiences. Cast members worked grueling twelve to eighteen-hour workdays on the sets and costumes, willingly jeopardizing their eyesight and overall health just to be a part of a Hibiscus spectacle. The sets and costumes were giant, lavish and gorgeous. They reflected the enormity of the venue and the ever-expanding budget. Brian's scripts called for

dancing horses, dancing poodles, people in huge feathered headdresses and an opulent staircase. Busby Berkeley and Georges Méliès would have been impressed.

The CEO-produced version of *Sky High* opened to horrifying revues, except for the New York Times. Reviewer John Corry wasn't crazy about the show but liked the fast action and had nice things to say about Hibiscus' sisters and their beautiful trio harmonies, ending with "Buried in *Sky High* is a sister act."

Although they had officially broken up and were no longer lovers, companions or even confidantes, Hibiscus and Angel Jack were still bickering. It was a very turbulent time for everyone. Adding to the chaos, the *Sky High* company was forced to move from the large Entermedia, a theater big enough to land a plane in, to the intimate, more accessible Players Theater on MacDougal Street in Greenwich

Village, with a stage the size of a handkerchief. Having to squeeze the large costumes and sets into that small house was nearly impossible.

Left to right: Eloise, Jayne Anne and Mary Lou in Sky High
at the Entermedia Theater, New York City, 1979

William Frothingham, aka Palm Spareengz

The other time and place I knew your brother was in New York City, five or six years later, probably 1978 or 1979. I had been out to dinner with Charlie Cowles, an acquaintance that I met here in Seattle. He was a gallerist, a native New Yorker, who had lived in Seattle a couple of years for professional reasons. We were joined at the restaurant by David Hockney, the painter. After dinner we all went to an infamous bar called Cowboys and Cowgirls, in Midtown on the East Side. It was pretty crowded and pretty noisy and I think we were standing at the bar. This fellow came over and was talking to David Hockney and he was introduced to me as "Brian O'Hara." He seemed so familiar. He might've had a blazer on and was really preppy looking - short hair, as was I – I had also totally changed my dress and my appearance.

He walked away for a moment. This Brian O'Hara just seemed so familiar. Charlie said, "Well, he used to be known as Hibiscus" – and it was one of those "You're kidding me!" moments. So that's how I made the reconnection with your brother in New York. Shortly thereafter he contacted me because he was starting pre-production for *Sky High*. Hibiscus was kind enough to invite me to some of the rehearsals in the loft. I met your sisters, and I'm pretty sure I met your mom also at that point. This was so exciting because it was a whole other side of your brother that I had no idea about when I met him in Seattle originally. I went to two different performances of *Sky High* and was so impressed because it had the look and aesthetic of a Cockettes show but probably a little broader commercial appeal – more polished, definitely. Those costumes were just so great. I was really impressed with your sisters, they were amazing, I mean, here they are, three beautiful, sexy extremely talented women with this great stage persona. Yeah, it was just so exciting for me to have seen Hibiscus go from The Palace Theater to the Angels of Light to … Broadway!

The weight of his job to keep his CEO-boyfriend happy (and interested) in addition to other benefactors around the globe required George to create and send amusing, elaborate, glitter-encrusted newsletters keeping his supporters abreast of where their money was going. But his heart was no longer in it. Brian was beginning to lose his sparkle, his twinkle and his charm. After all of these colorful and artistic years, theater was beginning to feel like work for him.

Although the new *Sky High* found a modest niche audience, including high profile New Yorkers like Andy Warhol and English royal Jamie Spencer-Churchill, Marquess of Blandford, who attended many times, Hibiscus was growing distressed and feeling lost. This *Sky High* was nothing more than a "greatest hits" pastiche of his past work. It was more polished for sure, with a budget, a staff and a theater in a great location, but Hibiscus' DNA was in short supply. The show lacked the organic, freewheeling spontaneity that was his stock in trade. Audiences, critics and eventually the cast considered it sterile and unrecognizable as George's signature work. As ticket sales plummeted and his underground "cred" was called into question, Hibiscus' embarrassment affected his behavior. Hiding behind the false identity of Brian O'Hara, Hibiscus was, for the first time, experiencing self-loathing.

Theater-as-commerce did not achieve the personal victory he had hoped for. He felt buried by rigid schedules, union rules and financial peril. His "golden handcuffs" became insufferable and drove him to the verge of a breakdown.

Wrap party for the cast of Sky High, New York City, circa 1979

Hibiscus was confronted with the fact that his renovated theater-du-jour was most certainly a flop, critically and financially and, worst of all, artistically. The notion that a cleaned-up, watered down version of his brand could meet the high threshold for success in tough-as-nails New York was a false premise and doomed to fail. Hibiscus was beginning to feel numb and broken. The intensity and fallout of giving up his dream of free theater in order to save the baby (the show) was beginning to wear on him.

Feeling his artistic compass was permanently broken, he began to reflect upon his greatest triumphs: the El Dorado Players in Clearwater, Florida and New York City; a successful solo theater career launched in the world's toughest proving ground; placing flowers in loaded guns during the 1967 March on the Pentagon which served as a lasting image of love, peace and flower power; his masterpieces, The Cockettes and The Angels of Light, where he championed free expression and provided a protected portal to a magical and safe place for anyone to show their most magnificent and self-actualized selves; and the triumphant European tours, where his work was celebrated as timely, socially relevant and politically impactful. These were his greatest achievements.

Hibiscus didn't just pave a road for men in glitter to dance around a stage; this was serious history in the making for gay rights, inter-gender collaboration and total free expression. His prior shows were an invited platform for those in need of safe passage to express who they were, regardless of gender, race or age. Hibiscus wanted to give his fellow brothers and sisters-in-arms the excitement of creative freedom, a spotlight, and the acceptance that society had denied.

Hibiscus' shows often recounted the history of the world. They turned on universal themes of good versus evil, coming of age, temptation and redemption. He cast himself as the hero, the victor, the rescuer and the savior of the enslaved and downtrodden souls who were in need of salvation and liberation. The shows often portrayed men in glitter who were also masculine, blending into a theatrical version of themselves as strong, authoritative, influential and triumphant beings.

Under the cloak of Brian O'Hara, Hibiscus was losing touch with who he was and what he stood for. His bright light was growing dim. He resolved to shake off his malaise and resume creating art that was new, revolutionary and in touch with the times.

APRIL 1980

Dear Jet,

You have inspired me once again. Free theatre will live! Manhattan will begin receiving free extravaganzas. The golden age will dawn once again!

In prisons, hospitals, senior gay AA meetings, feeding halls, senior citizens homes. To hell with queendom. With you and Sister Theresa as my guide my life will change.

I am putting it all
in motion. The costumes
and sets will come
at of stages.
Paid shows have brought
me nothing but misery
and debt. All for
art. The stage is
set ... on with
the show THIS
IS IT!

Love,

Hilary

Chapter 10
Hibiscus and the Screaming Violets
and *Tinsel Town Tirade*

Tossing off his golden handcuffs, Hibiscus' energy and imagination were back, bigger and better than ever. He was eager to meld his own theater style with the emerging new music culture in New York City.

Hibiscus, the new enigmatic glam-rocker. Photo by Irene Young, 1981

After *Sky High,* Hibiscus had limited funds with which to set his sights on new creative adventures. He hadn't a clue where the next installment of money would come from, and didn't care. He knew he had to start fresh, that his art came first, and that resources would materialize as needed. Pragmatists around him argued that he was wasting money and time. But Hibiscus was steadfast and firm in his ideals. He was a master at enduring the chorus of critics around him. Hibiscus reveled in his own ideas and theatrical style of living. He was the creator and engine of his own world, driven by his vision and insistence on finding and expressing his own voice. He found that he still had support from faithful friends and from patrons with whom he had not burned bridges.

The infamous Studio 54 dance club had opened and was the hot spot to be seen. Hibiscus and Angel Jack, now "just friends," made a steady habit of dressing in their finest drag and dancing the night away. On any given night one could find Andy Warhol, Diana Ross, Bianca Jagger, Liza Minnelli, Michael Jackson, Fran Lebowitz, the fashion designer Halston and so many more. The Studio 54 scene was filled with glamour, champagne, cocaine and sex in the balcony, bathroom and basement. A new euphoria was dawning!

At Studio 54, circa 1981

Hibiscus, at age 30, had already led many lives and had been through so much. He studied the rapidly changing landscape of New York's performance culture and music scene. The world was changing the way it viewed entertainment. The Music Television Videos network (MTV) launched its first broadcast and videos were the new rage. The music video scene was exploding with new stars and opportunities.

Robert Heide

At some point in the 1970s the legend of Hibiscus and The Angels of Light, The Cockettes and other far-out groups, some inspired by glitter rockers, found Hibiscus joining in on the fun and frenzy of it all by forming his own rock act which included his sisters Jayne, Eloise, and Mary Lou – and thus was born *Hibiscus and the Screaming Violets.*

179

Hibiscus felt tentative and a bit roughed up by his last money-fueled, hollow victory in commercial theater. He wanted his next adventure to be unique, yet authentic to his personality and his own vision. Wisely, he asked his friend Martin Worman to direct his new act. Martin, a tremendously talented actor, director and activist, had known Hibiscus since being a Cockette himself in San Francisco. Having a graduate

degree in theater, Martin had the depth of perspective to understand Hibiscus' unique talents and eccentricities. He agreed to direct, choreograph, write and stage Hibiscus' entry into New York City's exciting live music scene. Martin was very good for Hibiscus, and they made a powerful artistic combination.

Lance Loud and Martin Worman join Hibiscus and the Screaming Violets for a photo session atop their glittering billboard. Sheridan Square. Greenwich Village, 1981

Always one to put out the word, even before the act was ready, Hibiscus rented the giant, highly visible billboard above the Schulte Cigar Store, on Christopher Street in Sheridan Square, to advertise *Hibiscus and the Screaming Violets*. His billboard was lettered with thousands of sequins stitched in place by a sewing circle of elderly women in Brooklyn (according to Hibiscus). He gave them credit from the stage at the end of each show, a glam rock and roll act. The billboard, positioned in Greenwich Village's most visible spot, announced his new face and act to the world. Hibiscus was counting on his sisters to be The Screaming Violets in his new art-rock band. However, they were growing up and making lives of their own. They had already refused to be in his new show, *Tinsel Town Tirade*, which was slated to open at Theater for the New City, and starring Jackie Curtis (soon replaced by Holly Woodlawn) and George.

180

The Harris Sisters and Trouble.
Photo: Kenn Duncan, 1981

Paul and Miki Zone (Man 2 Man)
with The Screaming Violets at
Danceteria. Photo: Don Marino

Jayne Anne, Eloise and Mary Lou parted ways with Hibiscus after *Sky High* closed. After enduring Hibiscus' life-long teasing, dishing and shaming their developing womanhood, they decided enough was enough. They had been working at Studio 54 and had formed their own rock and roll band, *The Harris Sisters and Trouble, and* played most of the rock venues on the New York music circuit including CBGB, s.n.a.f.u., and Great Gildersleeves.

Hibiscus assumed that his sisters would drop everything and join him, as they always had – but this time they ignored his tactics and his invitation to join his new rock act, *Hibiscus and the Screaming Violets,* despite their mother's pleas to coax them. He was shocked and stunned when they declined. Not used to taking no for an answer, he mounted a campaign to win them back. He sent flowers, perfume and systematically showed up at their performances, jumped on stage and sang his "will you come with me?" song. Eventually convinced, they became his Screaming Violets. It wasn't until later they learned that he had included their names in all of his press releases and had already stolen their band away from them.

Hibiscus spent sleepless nights crafting his new persona. He looked to his younger brother Fred to arrange the music and lead the band. Fred assembled a versatile unit from among the best musicians on the rock-and-roll scene: Bill Davis, guitar; Ray Ploutz, bass; Mike Padulla, drums; with Fred as keyboardist, arranger and conductor. While Ann and Fred wrote new glitter-rock songs for the act, Hibiscus found rehearsal space and set out a plan to be ready for clubs and shooting a video for MTV. Soon his glitter-glam-rock quest was ready to hit the New York scene.

Poster created by Dave Simmons, 1981

Hibiscus and the Screaming Violets birthed a new and joyous Hibiscus. He was now a skilled overseer. He worked tirelessly with his team, director, Martin Worman, and with publicists John Carmen and the visionary Jane Friedman, to ensure success. In early 1981, *Hibiscus and The Screaming Violets* embarked on a tour of New York City dance clubs: Studio 54, Xenon, The Ice Palace, Danceteria, The Peppermint Lounge, Bonds, s.n.a.f.u. and The Red Parrot. *(1)*

George and company performed on the same music circuit as Madonna, Adam Ant, Michael Musto and The Must, The Weather Girls, and Cyndi Lauper. The underground punk clubs included The Mudd Club, The Bitter End, The Underground, and CBGB alongside Nona Hendryx, China Davis, Deborah Harry's Blondie, The Ramones, Grace Jones, Bobby Reed and Holly Woodlawn. Hibiscus, his Violets and their band found a weekly rock-and-roll home stage at Lewis Friedman's club s.n.a.f.u. on 21st Street and Avenue of the Americas.

182

Laurence Frommer

Cast member of *Hibiscus,* a 1992 biographical musical at La MaMa

I spent most of my youth with the "Hibiscus and Screaming Violets" billboard as a staple fixture of hilarity in my frantic

comings and goings. The picture even sustained me through "the beginning of the end" - the Reagan years, AIDS, and the religious right. What a strange nightmare this country has become since that billboard image disappeared! The absolute Par-tay that was Sheridan Square, and all of the "Villages - "East and West" - is no more! Funny, I still want to play and sing and feel the thrill and power that was Village Nights! I loved being part of your show and paying tribute to the long-lost image that sustained me as I saw America go crazy. (2)

Topman Magazine: Hibiscus Glitters the Lily, Photos by Irene Young, circa 1982 (3)

Don Marino

Friend and neighbor of Hibiscus in Greenwich Village

I met George through Lance Loud. They were very close friends and would call each other HONEYYY!! in a very loud high-pitched voice. George was living in a very cool loft on Greenwich Street or thereabouts. He had a little mini stage in the middle of the room with a glittery curtain and would rehearse his act "Hibiscus and The Screaming Violets." No one could ever forget the huge glittering sign over Village Cigars.

George and I once had a conversation about gossip. I remember being hurt by someone saying something about me and telling him I didn't like people saying derogatory things about me behind my back. "You don't?" he said. "I like that." I knew then and there he was from another planet, much more evolved than me. George liked black guys and he would say you could always depend on them and demonstrate with his hands a big dick.

Hibiscus' fun, gregarious friend and musical companion was **Lance Loud**. Lance was the first reality TV star – the eldest son in a family made famous by the groundbreaking cinema vérité series *An American Family*.

As the first openly gay person to appear on television, Lance was vilified by the media. But the American public loved him. Lance was an inspiration to legions of young people, both gay and straight, for daring to live his life on his own terms.

When one or the other was out of town, Lance and George maintained a lively banter via picture-postcards.

Lance and Hibiscus were best buddies through thick and thin. (4)

Paul Zone
Pioneering punk-rock bandleader of The Fast, musician, photographer and Hibiscus' friend. *Photo by R. Shay*

"I love talking about people and gossiping, don't you?" George would say in the sweetest and most playful way. He would pop up at the window of my ground floor Greenwich Village apartment (less than 2 streets from that GINORMOUS sparkling "Hibiscus" Sheridan Square Billboard) and sing in at the top of his lungs, *"I DON'T WANNA TALK,"* the opening line of ABBA's hit, "The Winner Takes It All" with news and gossip of the day.

My friends Lance Loud and Don Marino would sit around with me laughing uncontrollably as George would spin into the room like a tornado, or a shiny silver pinball, bouncing off the walls shouting out a play-by-play of his escapades from the day or night before. Screaming to get a word in edgewise was surely annoying to the neighbors: when George was around everyone's amps had to be turned up to 11. He was always "ON," and you loved him for that; loved to be around that puppy jumping all over you. Less than a handful of people that I've known have that built in magic. His memory has stayed with me and makes me smile to this day.

In Sheridan Square, Harris family archives, circa 1982

Hibiscus and his Screaming Violets were scheduled to record a three-song short album for a tour that Hibiscus had booked in Japan. They were interviewed by Robin Leach, host of television's *Lifestyles of the Rich and Famous,* and had a press junket on Fire Island. They were poised and ready for the big time!

Tinsel Town Tirade, Hibiscus' new musical, co-written with Penny Arcade, co-starring Holly Woodlawn and directed by rising television programming star Jeff Wachtel, opened at Theater for the New City, running simultaneously with *Hibiscus and the Screaming Violets.* Hibiscus performed at 8:00pm in *Tinsel Town Tirade*, changed his costume and ran to an 11:00pm (or later) rock show with Jayne Anne, Eloise, Mary Lou and Fred; then they taxied to Studio 54 so his sisters could work the night in the coat check and Hibiscus could network at the club. This grueling schedule repeated itself almost every night of the week. Hibiscus and his sisters would sleep most of the day to be able to keep up the pace. Ann supported them in every way she could. Like in the old days off-off Broadway, Ann wrote for the shows and cooked round the clock for her children.

Hibiscus (standing right), Holly Woodlawn (standing left), L to R sitting, Beth North, Patty Ben Peterson, Karen Wexler, 1982

Jayne Anne, Eloise and Mary were already fully booked with Hibiscus' dreams including *Hibiscus and the Screaming Violets* and the filming of his movie, *Hollywood Hotel*.

So when they turned down *Tinsel Town Tirade,* Hibiscus finally did what he had been threatening for years. He hired three other girls for the production and preceded to shower them with glamour, jewels, costumes, press … and love.

Holly Woodlawn and Hibiscus

187

WORLD PREMIER! ALL STAR CAST OF THE DECADE!

LIMITED ENGAGEMENT

THEATRE FOR THE NEW CITY
Bartineiff/Field
present

HOLLY WOODLAWN
in

TINSEL TOWN TIRADE

THE
NEW
MUSICAL
by
HIBISCUS

APRIL
2.3.4.8.9
10.11.15.16.17
11 p.m.

ALSO STARRING:

PENNY ARCADE · DON FADEAWAY · GIOVANI LUKE WARM
RICHARD BRUCE · AMES ENGELBERG · GRETTA GIANCARLO
BETH NORTH · PATTY BEN PETERSON · KAREN WEXLER
EVAN LEE SWINDLER · JOYCE MANDELL
HIBISCUS and the SCREAMING VIOLETS

DIRECTED BY: JEFFERY SHOCK
MUSIC & LYRICS: FRED & ANN HARRIS
SETS & COSTUMES: ANGEL JACK
CHOREOGRAPHY: LOULOU BELLE & ELOISE HARRIS

THEATRE FOR THE NEW CITY
162 Second Ave.
Info: 254-1109

Chapter 11
GRID

Ann Harris

It started with a whimper – a short article in the newspapers about a strange new illness among a small number of gay men. It was called Gay Related Immune Deficiency (GRID). It was associated with a high level of stigma and discrimination, because it was linked to the gay population. The government did not respond to the crisis, but in New York City, the Gay Men's Health Crisis organization came to the rescue of victims of the emerging epidemic.

Reports of discrimination against gay men with the virus were beginning to emerge. On top of handling new health challenges, they sometimes faced rejection by family and friends. They were often forced out of their homes, lost their jobs, and frequently became victims of violence. (1)

By 1982 Hibiscus had grown hungry for real affection. No longer satisfied by the casual lover, he longed for the type of love and devotion that only a real boyfriend could give. However, his capacity for companionship was so large that no one person could fill it. Hibiscus had already lived so many different lives and lifestyles, complete with diverse names, homes, clothing and personas. The multitude of developed parts of his personality each required something or someone different. His actor persona partnered with **Robert Tannanis**, a handsome, dapper commercial actor. Robert was well educated and was cast mostly in television soap operas and commercials. He helped Hibiscus maintain a healthy lifestyle, including nourishing food and a regular sleep schedule. A deeper love relationship was with longtime boyfriend Gary. Both kept their own separate homes but would vacation together in the Caribbean. It appeared to be more than a traditional boyfriend relationship. Gary grounded and calmed Hibiscus. However, when Gary had had enough of Hibiscus' erratic energy, compulsive wandering eye, and trouble focusing, and broke up with him, Hibiscus was devastated. He cried endlessly and played the song "Just Once" by James Ingram repeatedly. His friend Lance Loud provided a much-needed shoulder to cry on.

Hibiscus also felt an obligation to the wealthy CEO boyfriend who had paid for many of his opulent adventures. Long after Hibiscus was emotionally over this relationship, he continued to pretend, out of a feeling of debt. This was draining and sucked the life and joy out of his normally effervescent personality.

Hibiscus had a penchant for scenario sex (role-playing) and preferred diversity for his imaginative sexual appetite. His home was near the Hudson River in Greenwich Village and close to the notorious trucks where clandestine trysts between gay men would take place. Hibiscus visited the trucks for most of his New York life. It was hot, sweaty and dangerous but filled a tremendous hunger that dwelled in his psyche. The full extent of the danger was about to reveal itself.

Robert Heide

The ringing in of the new decade of the 1980s brought with it a frightening new disease, which seemed to target the gay community. At first it was called 'Gay Related Immune Deficiency' or 'GRID' and later 'Acquired Immune Deficiency Syndrome' or 'AIDS.' This plague as it was called and which was thought to have originated and spread through monkeys in Africa seemed like it might have come out of medieval times; but to be sure the party was at this juncture certainly over. Death was on the prowl and stalking everyone, everywhere just as in the Ingmar Bergman film *The Seventh Seal*. Was this disease 'the seal' of the seventies and was the decade of the eighties to be eventually referred to as 'the AIDies'? The answer is <u>YES!</u>

Adrian Milton

The next time I saw [Hibiscus] was at a party he gave at his loft. I met David McDermott and Peter McGough, the Time Traveling artists, who at that time were unknown but who are a big success today. Patrick and I visited them in Ireland this past autumn. It was around Valentine's Day, 1982. David sang along with an old Victrola and we became fast friends immediately. Hibiscus looked great at the party. He was going by the name Brian. The mother/daughter hooker team who were in *Luminous Procuress* were there. The mother/daughter team was trying to induce me to have a threesome with them to excite one of their older male clients who was getting tired of the same old routine.

A few days after the party I called to thank Hibiscus and there was no answer and no answering machine to leave a message on. I tried again a week later. When I spoke to Madeleine she said Hibiscus had the flu and could not kick it.

Quite suddenly, Hibiscus developed mysterious symptoms of a deep cough and significant weight loss. He quickly deteriorated to the point where his mother moved in to take care of him. Ann brought George his favorite foods – steak and lemon meringue pie (he had a voracious appetite yet could not hold anything down) – processed his ever-growing piles of laundry, cleaned his house and kept him company, while she held down a full-time job. They talked about his plans for future artistic endeavors.

Hibiscus may have had a sixth sense about his mortality, as he had never before executed so many projects simultaneously as *Tinsel Town Tirade*, *Hibiscus and the Screaming Violets*, *Hollywood Hotel;* and a new play he was writing, his first non-musical, *Summer's End*, about a romantic gay love affair, This unfinished play, along with song sketches he was working on, suggest that Hibiscus was retiring his purple crayon in favor of more serious writing.

Hibiscus and the Screaming Violets *gave one last triumphant performance on their home stage at S.N.A.F.U., after which George collapsed.*

One night, well into his illness, Ann called Eloise to tell her that his cough had gotten worse and he may not make it to the *Hibiscus and the Screaming Violets* show that night at Magique, the upper east side Manhattan discotheque. Eloise rushed to the venue, and found Jayne Anne, Mary Lou and the band in a state of confusion. "Hibiscus is late and we can't get a hold of him." In desperation they tried to think of who had the right range to sing in Hibiscus' keys (Michael Musto or Paul Zone of the Fast) just in case Hibiscus couldn't make it to the gig. Ten minutes before they were due on stage, Hibiscus burst through the door in full make-up, wig and costume. His mother held him up as he staggered to the stage. He was skinny and frail, but without hesitation gave a breathtaking, powerful, charismatic performance. All his stage powers and mastery of audience connection were engaged. His singing and movements were in perfect synch with his sisters, Fred and the band. With fire and fury, they rocked the house like there was no tomorrow.

With the crowd still screaming for more, he walked proudly off the stage and collapsed in an agonized state. Only his family knew just how sick he truly was, but they didn't doubt he would recover. He had been sick before and had bounced back from bouts of self-pity and weeks of depression.

Ann and Hibiscus made a pact that he would NOT go to the hospital under any circumstances. The reasons for this were a complicated mix of there being no previous model for his symptoms, absolute denial, Irish stubbornness, financial limitations, Ann's inclination to go along with George's wishes – and perhaps thinking they could cure him with magic and chicken soup.

Hibiscus, two weeks before going to St Vincent's hospital in Greenwich Village, 1982. Photo by Paul Zone

One day, while Ann was at work, Robert Tannanis visited him and got scared. Robert was horrified at Hibiscus' appearance. He had lost a tremendous amount of weight, had a raging fever and purple spots all over his body. He was able to tell Robert that he did not want to go to the hospital because he was going to get better. Robert wasn't listening. He said, "Pact, *shmact,* we are going to the emergency room." Robert carried Hibiscus to a taxicab. Through panic and tears he directed the driver, "St. Vincent's Hospital!"

Ann recounts how Robert, over the phone, described to her the chaotic scene unfolding at the hospital while waiting for a doctor:

Robert Tannanis, 1982

George could barely stand. I held him up and practically dragged him into the emergency room. He said his vision was blurry and what was happening seemed like a dream. I shouted, "Help him, please! Somebody, please bring a wheelchair!" I carried George to the triage nurse's station, burst into tears and screamed, "His name is George Harris! He has a rash all over his body! He can hardly breathe, has a fever and he has lost a lot of weight… his name is George Harris, please, please help him, *help him!"* A young man in scrubs brought a wheelchair. He smiled and said to George, "Don't worry man, we'll get you fixed up. You'll feel better soon." The attendant wheeled him to an over-crowded corridor where we waited hours just to be seen by a doctor. The emergency room was overflowing with men who had the same symptoms. After several agonizing hours, his name was finally called. As George was rolled down the corridor, I could hear machines beeping and whooshing. I noticed a man slumped over in a wheelchair, also bone-thin, with large purple blotches on his face and neck. The sights, sounds and smells of the hospital became intense. While George was being examined he began gasping for air. He became hysterical and shouted, "Oh my God, Robert, I can't breathe, I can't *breathe!!"*

194

Hibiscus was admitted to St. Vincent's Hospital. Just before he was placed on a ventilator, he asked Robert to give his mother a note that he had scribbled with the purple crayon he loved to write with. As a little kid back in Bronxville, George loved the book *Harold and the Purple Crayon* in which Harold, a small boy, could draw anything with his purple crayon, and it would become real – stairs, trees, the sun, moon and stars. George's note indicated that, if something were to happen to him he was leaving his Greenwich Village loft to her.

Hibiscus' doctors told his family that he had pneumocystis pneumonia, inflammation and fluid build-up in the lungs, and Kaposi's sarcoma, an opportunistic cancer caused by a weakened immune system. The doctors, and no one, yet knew that this was the beginning of the AIDS epidemic that would eventually reach global proportions. Robert made plans with Hibiscus' family to get together the following week. But by Monday, Robert was dead. His death was caused by an opportunistic brain infection due to a suppressed immune system. No one anticipated the brutality and swiftness of the HIV virus.

Don Marino

> When he got sick none of us had ever had any idea of what
> he had. We went to see him at the house and he was very
> weak. By the time he was in the hospital he had blown up like
> a frog and was out of it but I asked him if he knew I was there
> and he shook his head. That was the last time I saw him.

Adrian Milton

> [Hibiscus] was in St. Vincent's Hospital. I went to see him and
> he was unable to speak. It turned out he had pneumocystis
> pneumonia (which there was no remedy for at that time). His
> face was all blown up and swollen with liquids and he could
> only nod. His face was filled with pain and frustration. He took
> a brown paper bag and wrote me a note, but it was unreadable.
> We embraced and I left.

195

Michael Musto
Hibiscus' friend, fellow artist and writer. *Photo: Andrew Werner*

I was blissfully ignorant of The Cockettes' history when Hibiscus swept into town with a train of glitter behind him everywhere he went. But he was pushed down my throat, as it were by a frisky publicist, and I was immediately enchanted by his charm, his dazzle, and his innate sweetness. He was so much nicer than the other people being thrust at me! What he'd done on the other coast didn't matter to me since I was suddenly face to face with a force of nature that was lighting up my own town in the present moment. I not only covered his glam rock cabaret shows, but we performed on the same circuit (I had a Motown cover band), and in him, I found a kindred spirit with whom I could laugh at the absurdities of the scene while jointly appreciating the joys of being an underground NYC icon of the night. When Hibiscus got sick, I took his family's advice and ran to the hospital to rub his leg and send him good vibes. It was so not me –but it felt so right, and I was glad I got to say goodbye to a wonderful friend.

Many wonderful people, people who adored Hibiscus for his art, charisma and friendship, came to the hospital to visit him. He couldn't talk with the ventilator in place, so he wrote notes to the colorful parade of visitors. His family drove to the airport to pick up medicine sent by the Centers for Disease Control in Atlanta. Nothing seemed to help; in fact the medicine seemed to exacerbate his condition.

Hibiscus' family received a lot of support and comfort from a friend, Edward Oleksak, who had dedicated his life to escorting young men

196

home to lend support while they came out to their families, and/or broke the news that they were infected with the HIV virus. According to Edward, it didn't always go well. More often than not, both he and the young man in question would be rejected and asked (sometimes violently) to leave the premises. Edward would then work with a variety of social workers to provide housing, food and medical care to these young, frightened sick men.

The family had been taking turns being at Hibiscus' bedside. But on May 6, 1982, each one felt called to be there, as if he had summoned them individually. The playwright Harry Koutoukas, a close family friend, was there as well. As the machines clanged and beeped an unsympathetic doctor, new on the case, came in and said, "Not all of you should be in the room at once. What is this, a death watch?" Hibiscus' nurse gruffly chased him out. Fred leaned down to his ear and said, "George, I know it's just too much for you. We're all here and it's OK if you want to leave. We all love you." Hibiscus opened his eyes and looked at each person, then closed his eyes tightly as if he were going on a trip. His essence seemed to float around for a beat – then flew out the open window. Everyone present felt and saw it. Stunned, they sat silent awhile, a moment that felt like forever.

Harry Koutoukas looked toward the window and asked, sincerely, "Won't you reconsider?"

Mary Lou and Ann stayed in George's apartment that night. After they had fallen asleep, Mary Lou awoke and saw something swaying back and forth next to one of his tall plants. She tried to wake her mother with no success. Soon after, George's face and body appeared ... a bit cloudy, but a distinct form. Mary Lou said George was reaching his hands out to her. In a regretful moment of panic, she told him to go and he faded away. She spent decades hoping he would appear again so she could respond differently.

Hibiscus' memorial was held at Danceteria where the club's manager, Jim Fouratt, had originally offered to hold a benefit for Hibiscus' medical costs. Instead it became his last theatrical celebration. A host of performers, friends and family sang and spoke about George, his life, and how his presence had enriched their lives. The memorial ended with a spotlight on a microphone onstage with his boots and cape. Hibiscus' voice came over the sound system singing his last recorded song, a disco version of "A Whiter Shade of Pale."

Over the years, many artists and friends have joined him in paradise.

Hibiscus' memorial at Danceteria: The Screaming Violets and the cast of Tinsel Town Tirade *including Penny Arcade and Holly Woodlawn. Photos by Charles Moniz, 1982 (2)*

Denise Ryan

Journalist based in Vancouver, B.C. recounts a story from colleague and gay archivist **Ron Dutton**

A couple of years ago I did an in-depth series on the Emergence of AIDS in Vancouver in the 1980s and how it affected the community. Vancouver, BC, where I now live, was the place where the anti-retro viral triple cocktail that became the gold standard for treatment and effectively changed the prognosis for patients around the globe was developed.

My reason for doing the story was personal: like so many who lived through the 80s and lost close friends, I remembered the fear, the panic and the mistreatment of patients, in particular, gay men. I wanted people to remember; I think it's urgent that we do so that it never happens again.

My first experience with what was then called GRID was when I arrived in New York to go to school and my aunt, Liz Ryan, asked me to accompany her to a memorial for Hibiscus, the son of close family friends. It was at Danceteria.

I had never met him.

I remember how empty the cavernous room was, the combination of nightclub's colored lights and long shadows, the whispered discussions about "GRID" and then, suddenly, the performance of his sisters onstage, glorious, exuberant, tears running down their faces. And behind them a slide show of family photos including the LIFE Magazine photo of George putting the flower in the barrel of a gun.

How many times had I stared at that photo leafing through the LIFE Magazine book of photos that had been in our living room as a kid growing up in Canada? That image, so iconic, that gesture so pure.

I never forgot that night either, and years later, when thinking about that era, aware that so many moments of personal and historical significance were being left behind, I was struck by the connection I had always held in my imagination and in my

199

heart, of that photo of a beautiful boy, and his loss later in one of the darkest chapters of social history. For me, they were always intertwined. How brave some people can be, even if the battle is desperately unfair, flowers against guns.

That enduring recollection of Hibiscus was part of the impetus for me to write the series, *Heroes, Heartbreak and Hope: How AIDS Made Us Better,* to remember those who were lost, what we collectively lost, and the others who fought to save them.

As I was researching, I told this story to Ron Dutton, who is a volunteer keeper of the Gay archives in this city.

He looked at me kind of strangely as I was describing Hibiscus, what little I knew of him, as the seed of my quest to preserve and honor some of this history.

Dutton told me how some time in his youth he had been travelling in Greece. He was in a small town — one of those whitewashed seaside towns, when over the hill came a man trailing flowers and glitter, an eruption of color and music, along with some troubadours, a spectacular sight. He was quite sure it was Hibiscus. He didn't remember much more than that, except that it was glorious.

And he shared that moment with me.

I felt, as we were talking, that all of Hibiscus's bright beauty and loveliness was there in the room with us and had survived like a piece of music does, to play against the shadows.

Devastated by Hibiscus' death, his sisters grappled with the challenge of rebuilding their lives, which had been on hold since youth, under George's influence. Having been conditioned with glitz and adventure, it hadn't yet dawned on them that they could take charge and venture out on their own. Hibiscus' glittery world was all that had mattered for three decades. With heavy hearts, they began to map out new lives with fresh ideas and self-determination, going to college, dating and mating, having families and choosing careers.

Ann, also devastated and newly confronted with a life threatening thyroid condition, perhaps triggered by the stress of Hibiscus' illness and death, became a new focal point for the Harris sisters' time and attention. Helping their mother process what the greatest blow of her lifetime, was now of the utmost importance.

Epilogue

On the night of May 6, 1982, Hibiscus' light went out....

How do you deal with the death of someone who braved the darkness and violence to find their voice, their strength, their purpose and their light in which to dance – in order to be seen by the world? Someone who has given you that opportunity too?

Many people were affected by Hibiscus' death. He encouraged everyone who crossed his path and gave them a stage to be what they wanted to be. His journey was intertwined with actualizing his own dreams while simultaneously lighting the road for others to actualize theirs. He illuminated a freely expressive, gay glittering path for others to follow or be empowered by. Ultimately, the world is inspired and enriched because of Hibiscus and the human flowers around him. His legacy is one of freedom of expression – and a social hunger and connectedness that revealed itself through his creativity, his special forms of theater and his unique way of being.

George Harris III had few inhibitions. He was completely natural, gregarious and fun; personality characteristics that were mesmerizing and contagious. Never able to be harnessed or conditioned by society, he empowered those around him through music, dance, fashion, make-up, free expression, Technicolor visuals and a chance at stardom.

Hibiscus was the inspirer and driver who coaxed creativity and elicited cooperation from all who chose to join his merry band. Family, friends, acquaintances and cast members worked well into the night and through long weekends in exchange for the opportunity to be part of his creative tribe. Having lived through the raucous hippie and artistic global transformations of the 1960s and 1970s, and having traveled widely through Europe with its ancient roots, Hibiscus was influenced by nature, culture, religion, sex, money and raging societal revolutions. He poured everything he experienced into his theater.

Hibiscus was rebellious, living by his own rules and adolescent dreams. He consciously advocated for the underdog. As if he were the love child of Don Quixote and Cinderella, he would cast ordinary people in his shows and transform them into extraordinary performers. Hibiscus turned rags into gowns and sent his new stars to the Ball. He was drawn to creative spirits and people who were often overlooked by society. He sprinkled glitter on them and filled their hearts and souls with stardust. The transformations were incredible and unforgettable to both audiences and performers.

This all came from a blank stage and an imaginative mind. Through his art, creativity and heart, in combination with his fearlessness and nerves of steel, Hibiscus achieved his life's dream and along the way inspired new forms of theater, film, literature, fashion, music, art and politics.

The brave, peace-seeking teenage boy, who gently placed flowers in the barrels of loaded guns, and Bernie Boston's perfect photograph capturing that extraordinary moment in time, have inspired millions to choose peaceful protest to effect social change. In this, the fiftieth anniversary year of the demonstration at the Pentagon, the power of that image continues to speak to the thousands marching for peace, equality and justice in the streets today.

The NAMES Project Foundation
AIDS Memorial Quilt Archive

CERTIFICATE of AUTHENTICITY

Quilt Block Number: **00069**

This print has been produced by the AIDS Memorial Quilt Archive
from the permanent photographic record of the Quilt.
This Quilt section was photographed on Kodak film according to
the highest professional standards and printed using Kodak digital
printing equipment and paper.

The mission of the NAMES Project Foundation
is to use the AIDS Memorial Quilt to help bring an end to the AIDS epidemic.

Anthony Turney
Executive Director
and Chief Executive Officer

Cleve Jones
Founder

ENCORE!
One Rhinestone - A Thousand Ripples

Ann Harris - *Photo by Charles Caron*

I know first-time experiences are special. My girlfriends and I always compared notes and the biggest and best was always the birth of our first child. With no experience whatsoever, "me" became "we" in a moment. When Georgie was born the doctor came in to congratulate me. He told me "We had an awful time getting that little fellow to breathe," imagine. Did I pay more attention because of that? I found out later with three boys and three girls they were all different – almost as if they came from totally different places and were loved by totally different people, and now it was my turn to find the pieces of the puzzle they were missing. I hope I succeeded because I am proud of them all and grateful to them for choosing me.

The first two little boys, Georgie and Walter, were inseparable, almost as if they knew each other from another world. They shared everything with each other including thoughts. Anyway, as each child came along it seems as if he or she was educating me about life, not the other way around, and fantasy was my second name. Fun comes in there too.

To get back to George, he was so easy to write songs for because it seems he liked and used everything I wrote in his shows. If he didn't have a scene that fit the song, he made one up for the next show. No wonder I got "too big for my britches." Lots of times he would pass by me singing the Barry Manilow tune "She Writes the Songs," anyway, "those were the days."

Differences of opinion were rarely about the work. Most of the time it would be a letter, "Mom, keep the songs coming in." He traveled a lot. Who could keep up? After he died we would hear the door of his Greenwich Street loft slam and look at one another and say or think "That's George." There is no way to describe his loss. Each in their own way relives fun times or events that we had with him. He made each one of us feel like the only child, like – "I'm the favorite."

George Harris, Sr.

Photos: left, Michael Ian; Right, George Harris Sr., Christopher Reeve and David Baxt in the 1978 movie Superman. © Warner Brothers, courtesy CapedWonder.com

"When I played God in *Sky High*, having worked in many shows where I learn my lines, I'm given the blocking and everything else – I said to Hibiscus, "What do you want me to do?" "Anything you want, Dad." I said, "Well, you got an idea how you want me to play this?" "Oh, no, anything you want to do!" "How 'bout the makeup?" "Anything you want." And so that's the way I did, you know, I got my idea, and I did it! He never came to me as a director will, and say, "I think you should consider incorporating this, changing that." He'd let you do anything you wanted to do. And it was amazing. He just had the fun of putting on a show. I've seen this sometimes in theater – a moment of pure magic. But with him, it's the whole show."

206

Susan Dale Rose – *Hibiscus' first cousin*

My mother, Susan Joyce (Harris) Weimer, died in 2016. She was a painter of regional renown and managing her body of work required focus. I spent long hours reading documents and assessing and culling drawings, watercolors and paintings to create a distilled compilation of her work.

Often, just as I was thinking that I could not make my eyes study another of her wild and passionate pieces, I would come across a letter or a postcard from G3, whom we grew up calling Georgie. "Dear Aunt Susan," these notes began, and in a sprawl of his slashing, calligraphic script he would describe his latest adventure.

There were far more of these notes and letters than I would ever have expected. My mother kept them all, and they formed a chronology of sorts, connecting her vision of a time with his. Between the pages of her journal for 1965 I would find a showbill Georgie had sent her. In a sketchbook from 1971 there was a note scribbled on the bottom of a review. In the early 80s, alongside his last postcard to her, she wrote in furious inkmarks: "How does a young man die of pneumonia in New York City in this day and age? SOMETHING IS WRONG!"

Suddenly it made sense that in 2013, approaching 90 years of age, Mom had flown from her home in Albuquerque to Denver to see the West of Center traveling exhibit that featured Georgie's stunning journal. There had been an unsuspected connection between these two edge-dwelling artists, a link that was perhaps part blood and part deep affinity.

There were dozens of these notes and cards scattered through her papers, each one carefully inserted into a passage of time. This was a relationship I had not suspected, a loyalty I had not seen, a kinship I envied. Each one gave me a little spark of energy to carry on with my task of curatorship, and each one made me love my cousin a little more.

Sometimes I think he is still somewhere around, laughing and distracting and opening up our cages to seek our freedom.

Walter Michael Harris

While sifting through "the bins," as Mary Lou calls the mountains of family memorabilia in our family's archives, I found draft sketches for a new song Hibiscus had scribbled into one of his many spiral notebooks. The lyrics reveal that, near the end of his life, George was beginning to examine serious social issues in a non-satirical way. The following was to be a duet between gay lovers, one black and the other white:

Photo: Andrew Sherwood

In the state of this Nation
We got double discrimination
Being gay and black is a heavy load to bear
Do we dare?

(in harmony)
Double Discrimination
Double Discrimination
From the land where oranges grow
Double Discrimination
Double Discrimination
This man that I love is my beau

For we teach their children
And garden their yard
And fight at the fort
And judge them in court

Double Discrimination
All across the Nation

Double Discrimination
All across the Nation

In another sketch, George bemoans indignities suffered by gays at the hands of the In Crowd, or Jet Set, who depend on gays for so much:

The "In" Crowd's forgiving, for
Eccentricities are chic.

But then who would dress them
And fluff up their hair?
And mix up their perfumes
Perform in the shows
Decorate their houses
File their toes?

Design all their parties
Arrange all their flowers
Create all their rooms
And set all their styles?

They're witty, you know
Such ravishing escorts
Wherever you go.

The shows you see
On the Great White Way
Were probably written
By someone gay

And probably performed by someone gay
Choreographed, directed and more
I bet they wrote the bloody score…

These sketches show George moving away from fantasy and satire in favor examining injustices and intolerance that he experienced as a gay man. This bold new turn begs the question: would his future plays and musicals have shifted into a mode of social consciousness and protest?

The Cockettes, *a critically acclaimed documentary co-directed by* **David Weissman** *and* **Bill Weber.** *Strand Releasing June 28, 2002*

Weissman and Weber (see bios) delivered a fantastic documentary that shows in loving color much of what you've read here. Through first person interviews, still photos, music and archival footage the story of Hibiscus and the Cockettes comes alive on the screen.

"Just when you thought there was nothing fresh to know about the counterculture, along comes The Cockettes, a funny, triumphant, and moving documentary about the mad theatrical troupe of San Francisco upstarts who dared to be fab and flamboyant and gay and glam before even the late-'60s generation knew what to make of them…. takes you closer than just about any movie has to what was once really meant by the term "free-spirited.""

— Owen Gleiberman, Entertainment Weekly, July 10, 2002 (1)

"An irresistible documentary look at the ensemble of the moment in the hippie kingdom of San Francisco, this comprehensive and charming film not only recalls those days exactly, it also manages the wonderful trick of taking us back there along with it."

— Kenneth Turan, Los Angeles Times, July 26, 2002 (2)

Promo postcard for The Cockettes, *Clockwise from upper left are Jilala (James Tressler), John Waters, Marshall Olds, Fayette Hauser, Scrumbly and Dusty Dawn.*

With his shimmering charisma and outlandish pied-piper quality, Hibiscus ignited the original spark, attracting other like-minded creative people. The original Cockettes were instrumental in allowing Hibiscus to shine his brightest light and to express himself freely. Hibiscus and his creative partners seemed to have found the "magic beans" in the fairy tale. The free-spirited, gender-bending nature of Hibiscus' original idea inspired artists such as Sylvester, John Waters and Divine. Golden memories like those revisited in *The Cockettes* film recall a watershed time when gender bending, androgyny and cross-dressing had not yet found acceptance in American culture.

Holly Woodlawn - Actress
Co-author of *A Low Life in High Heels.* Photo: Hibiscus' archives

I began rehearsals for another off-Broadway show, *Tinsel Town Tirade,* which starred a friend of mine named Hibiscus. During the last week of rehearsal, Hibiscus caught a cold. We thought nothing of it, assuming he would shake it by opening night. A week later, however, he still had the cold, and when the play opened his condition worsened. He had gone to a doctor and was taking antibiotics, but they didn't seem to help.

Hibiscus kept getting weaker and weaker, but he refused to miss a show. This was his baby and he wasn't about to desert it. Determined to perform, he was at the theater every night, but whenever he finished a scene, he walked offstage into the wings and covered himself with a blanket because he had the chills. We were all very concerned, but he still refused to check into a hospital. Finally, he had no choice, as he had developed pneumonia.

A stand-in replaced him and the show went on. Two days later I went to visit him in the hospital and I was horrified. He was plugged into all of these strange machines, one that fed oxygen and another that monitored his heart and yet another that fed him antibiotics. It was like walking into a space ship. Two days later he died and the play closed. He was only 32.

All of a sudden, I started hearing stories about all these gay boys who are dying of pneumonia. It seemed to happen overnight. No one really knew what to think. We had no idea what was causing this to happen. It was as if a strange plague had struck. (3)

William Frothingham, aka Palm Spareengz

When I first met Hibiscus, I was really in awe. He was like this superstar in my world and so having been given the chance to actually meet the person too was really fulfilling. I was a few years younger and definitely a lot more naïve than a lot of my contemporaries at that time. In my experience with Ze Whiz Kidz, there were elements of the world we created and lived in that were kind of destructive and unhealthy. But both Hibiscus and Tomata du Plenty helped keep me on a more positive track, and that was certainly Hibiscus' nature.

After I initially met your brother in that period between Seattle and Europe, I had gone to the University of Washington and studied for a few years, which was good for me, to get into a more regimented sort of life. But that crazy Bohemian part of who I am affected everything that I did, moving forward from that point – so it was great to see Hibiscus again in New York and see how he had evolved and changed, as I had also.

I really think the whole Angels of Light/Cockettes era would not have had the same trajectory if it hadn't been for your brother's influence and guidance. I think that could have all happened, but – I don't know – it might not have gotten broadcast this far. I don't think it would've had the legs – or "wings" – if not for him.

Michael Varrati
Interview with writer/director/actress **Geretta**
Reprinted from Peaches Christ's Drag Dossier #2

> **Mchael Varrati preamble:** Geretta knew Hibiscus in New York in the days following his departure from The Cockettes. Geretta, who became a horror icon for her roles in films like Lamberto Bava's *Demons* and Lucio Fulci's *Murder Rock*, had an early start performing with Hibiscus on the Warhol-inspired stages of the Big Apple.

MV: That brings us to the New York years. Geretta, you worked with Hibiscus in the Theater for the New City's production of *Tinsel Town Tirade*. Can you tell me a little bit about the production?

Geretta: Hibiscus wrote the play, with collaboration from Penny Arcade [Warhol superstar & punk icon]. A lot of it was based on real people from The Factory. Holly Woodlawn was in the show too, and she also contributed a lot of her own dialogue, but the play was obviously meant to be scripted and not an improv piece. So a lot of that came from Hibiscus. He and his sisters of "Hibiscus and The Screaming Violets" also had several musical numbers, along with some other cast members. However, I can't sing, so I was out of those!

You mention "gender outlaws," but if I'm correct, the only person other than Hibiscus who could qualify as one of those in our show was Holly. The rest of us were young, run of the mill, primarily straight thespians doing our first play in New York. There were some boys liking boys, and boys being girls, but that wasn't the whole focus of the show. I say this because we were "legit" theatre and proud of it. At the time there was a lot of crap being called "theatre," darling, but we actually were, if you get my drift.

MV: Was *Tinsel Town Tirade* the first time you had met Hibiscus?

Geretta: I met him on the play. When it was first cast, it had a different name, but he couldn't get clearance for it, so he finally called it *Tinsel Town Tirade.* I used to audition for just about everything they did at The Theater of the New City and this was just one of the shows listed on the casting board. I showed up and I was cast as "Jayne Champagne."

Coincidentally, it always pissed me off, because people thought I was a boy playing a girl pretending to be Jayne Mansfield,
when in fact, I was a black girl pretending to be a white Jayne Mansfield. See the difference? That's talent. *–laughs--*

MV: You told me that you once tried to convince Hibiscus to have sex with you? How did that work out?

Geretta: For some reason that I no longer remember, we (he, another guy from the show, and I) had all gone out and spent the night at a guy's flat on 9th Avenue. This was way before that side of New York had any style. It was just cheap. I think Bruce Willis was still a bartender on 8th Avenue at the time. Anyway, we never did it. He smiled, kind of smirked, and said "I just like to watch." I think he and the other fellow would have been more suited to each other, anyway. I often think how my life would have been different after any sex act between us. He was pretty full blown [AIDS] by then, but none of us knew that at the time. I do, however, think he was listening though, while the other guy and I did it. Oh, to be 19 again! – *laughs–*

MV: Hibiscus was at the forefront of the AIDS crisis, being one of the first reported on individuals to succumb. Do you remember what your reaction was? Can you comment on his passing and the greater crisis to come?

Geretta: Well, on the ground floor, you don't know a "crisis is coming." I moved out of the States around 1980, so the true horror of it all…friends dropping like flies… I missed. I wish I had been there. I wish I could have done more. We lost an entire generation; they were completely gone, like after a war. We don't have those people to add to the general growth of the arts, nation, science, everything. You don't have their offspring. It's unimaginable. I wonder what the world would have been like without the epidemic. But, that's like wondering what the world would have been like 200 years ago without plague, famine, or war. A better place, surely, but not possible. I don't know. Maybe it's all a Matrix and somebody fucked up, pushed the wrong button and the whole system got a virus and we have to keep redoing all this until we get it right. It's spooky and scary. But, let's hope that one day it is a disease that will be cured, like many that were of epidemic proportions in the distant past. Hopefully it will no longer exist in the very near future.

How I found out about Hibiscus though, was a friend of mine sent me the New York Times article in Paris announcing Hibiscus had died from an unknown disease. I mean, this was when there really was no info at all yet.

A couple of years ago I ran into Penny Arcade and we just shook our heads. We said to each other, "He was like the first case publicized, right?" (4)

Penny Arcade

Performance Artist, Advocate and Activist; cast member in *Tinsel Town Tirade* - photo provided by Steve Zehentner

I met Hibiscus in November of 1981 when Jackie Curtis introduced me. I had become familiar at that time with Hibiscus's performance presence in NY but I knew little of his history with The Cockettes, etc. having spent most of the 70's outside of NY.

Hibiscus cast me as the Warhol superstar Ultra (nothing to do with Ultra Violet) in *Tinsel Town Tirade.* In the course of our rehearsals, I would imitate Andrea Whips Warhol, once a mutual friend of Jackie and mine, (who had suicided in 1972), to amuse Jackie and I found it easier to make statements about the gentrification I found in NY post '60s in her voice, it also seemed to annoy people less. Soon Hibiscus approached me and said, "What you are improvising is better than the part I wrote. Would you consider doing this in the show?" I was stunned. I spoke to Jackie about it and Jackie advised me to ask for a writer's credit in the program. I was terrified to ask Hibiscus as I really wanted to perform Andrea in *Tinsel Town,* but Jackie forced me, And when I approached Hibiscus he was very encouraging and said, "Yes, you deserve a writing credit." I do not exaggerate when I say that this was one of the most supportive acts that would take place in the history of my career because while I have always been a talented performer owing to circumstances in my early life I had very little emotional self-confidence.

216

Shortly afterwards, Hibiscus fired Jackie who was drinking heavily and missing rehearsals and he replaced Jackie with Holly Woodlawn, another old friend and cohort from our days in the Playhouse of The Ridiculous and Warhol's Factory. Sometime in early February, Hibiscus had a huge shock when his married boyfriend and patron dropped dead on a tennis court I believe in Puerto Rico and the funds suddenly dried up. This boyfriend had paid for the large sequined (!!!) Billboard of Hibiscus and The Screaming Violets on Sheridan Square, his fabulous apartment, etc. and Hibiscus became very stressed. Just after this, during rehearsals, we started to notice that a sore on his upper lip didn't seem to heal and then it developed what can only be described as a fungus or mold. Hibiscus who was a paradigm of energy seemed to be wasting away. At first I thought it was depression due to the loss of his boyfriend and at one point I said "Hibiscus, you don't have to die" because I saw Thanatos, death in his eyes but it hadn't yet occurred to me or anyone else that the specter of 'Gay Cancer" or GRID that had started to arise was affecting Hibiscus. One Sunday brunch, the ingénue in the show, Ames Engelberg, described Hibiscus's symptoms to her brother, then a resident doctor at NYU. He told Ames to tell Hibiscus to come and see him, "Tell Hibiscus I can help him," and he told Ames all about this plague that was rising in NYC among gay men.

By this time we were in performances at Theater For The New City. *Tinsel Town Tirade* was a great success among the public but we started to see Hibiscus's energy flagging and finally starting to fail onstage. It was a truly bizarre and spectral experience to see this dynamic performer barely able to make it thru the show—but Hibiscus refused to go to the doctor and nothing seems to convince him to. Finally, he could not leave the house and eventually I don't remember who brought him to St Vincent 's Hospital. I visited him there, now in a coma, surrounded by his distraught family. Being early in the AIDS epidemic, we had no idea what was happening and still hoped for a full recovery.

Many of us from the cast visited Hibiscus at St Vincent's but soon the horrific scene of Hibiscus's illness was to be repeated daily, over and over as our many friends became ill. In early May, Hibiscus died without ever regaining consciousness. His death was first to be described as AIDS instead of GRID.

George Harris III was born in a show business trunk. He had a tremendous idealism and charisma as well as a large and loving and supportive family of whom he had become the defacto creative leader, after the long example of his parents, George and Ann. Hibiscus bridged the Gay Theatre and Cabaret scenes of the late 70's and early 80's. At the time of his death shortly before his 33rd birthday, Hibiscus already had a long and storied performance history, having created The Cockettes, using the examples of Jack Smith's [film] *Flaming Creatures* which he had been exposed to at the Kaliflower Commune by Irving Rosenthal, and by his knowledge of Jackie Curtis and of The Playhouse of The Ridiculous in NY.

Hibiscus created The Angels Of Light after he was unceremoniously ousted from The Cockettes. Like so many other originators who were felled by AIDS it is impossible to imagine what he may have created had he lived.

Laurence Gartel
Digital Art pioneer

Thinking about the Angels of Light puts my brain skills to the test. After all it was 45 years ago while attending High School of Music & Art at the old castle building on 135th Street and Convent Avenue. It was at a time when my artistic skills were minimal but budding and impressions of life were new.

I am writing this as the Supreme Court just passed gay marriage in June 2015. We as humans have to allow others to be, act and love in their own way and their own manner.

This is what I was exposed to 45 years ago: One day, my dear friend Jayne Anne asked me to come to an off-Broadway play. It was something very different. Hibiscus with his long blonde hair, love

218

beads and long Indian type garb was a Jesus like figure singing in a way that opened new vision.

It was truly the "Angels of Light." Positivity. Hibiscus was ahead of his time and his performance, presentation and ideology could only be appreciated by those that were open to mind expansion. Right, wrong or otherwise, Art provides the intangible aesthetic to uplift the human spirit. To a young artist this performance was highly impressionable.

I am sure Hibiscus would be both happy and sad with today's world. Let us concentrate on victory today. What Hibiscus was advocating became reality just the other day. His message of love and acceptance has come to fruition. I can only conclude with my own assessment of that day and the impact it had on me. – It allowed me to be a more open, caring person. Letting in the Light, enforces me to create great Art.

Carol Dean
"This is HIBISCUS" (aka George Harris)

The impact of his work can be plainly seen in every drag show of our current era (RuPaul would be the first to admit the influence of Hibiscus) all the way through all aspects of show biz, disco and even PUNK. He was a true visionary and powerful cultural monkeywrencher.

Lendon Sadler

Hibiscus personified for me a whole phantasmagorical cosmos in a particular place and time. Now that reality has evolved, as life continually does, I have had the distance of a generation to reflect upon the dream world your son/brother wove about our coterie of extraordinary collaborators in the space that once was San Francisco.

Aging necessitates awakening to a broader understanding of life than youth can afford. For some of us the grandeur of that experience has been both a hallowed and traumatic history with which to contend. The pandemic deeply devastated our clan, mercilessly eviscerating the demigods of our youth before our eyes. It was almost unbearable. But we live on.

So it is a privilege to recall the shaman who conjured a vision that enchanted me, swept me up in a maelstrom that I shall not pretend to completely grasp even now. Truth be told, to paraphrase Jilala (a fellow Cockette), I was only part of the dusky heavenly backdrop that illuminated the wondrous star personas with which we were blessed. Hibiscus was the Sun. But each of us has a unique perspective that is valuable. I thank you for the opportunity to remember that era of laughter, lightning, and light.

Bobby Reed
Cabaret singer, actor, friend

The Harris family and I were all clearly on a similar path in New York to do shows and be creative and get on stage to sing and dance. That was pretty much our total focus and motivation. I had done a cabaret act since arriving in Manhattan in 1974, so Jayne Anne, Eloise and Mary Lou began singing with me on some of my club gigs (West Bank Café was one of our recurring spots), and George [Hibiscus] would come and support. He was always in the background at these events, letting his sisters be the focal point.

Then, through the fog of the 70s and 80s, I remember their *Hibiscus and the Screaming Violets* billboard above Sheridan Square. That was very impressive (no club acts of that era had billboards as I recall), and I remember their gigs at Lewis Friedman's s.n.a.f.u. on Sixth Avenue. Glittering and fabulous, George certainly was a showman. Their costumes had more sequins than a Vegas showgirl. That was their gig, when glitter drag rock was a genre. The audiences loved their shows. Jump to the dark days of the early 80s (before AIDS even had a name) and this one memory that will never leave my mind. Eloise told me George was in St. Vincent's with a mysterious illness, and we went there. I had just read a piece in The New York Times about a new illness striking gay men in San Francisco and New York. George was intubated on a respirator and unable to speak. He gave a little note to one of the girls, [written to his ex-boyfriend] and on it read: "Call Gary, make it [sound] worse [than it is]." As if the new AIDS wave needed to be made worse. The dark humor in that small moment has never left me. I think it illustrated George's unflinching optimism. Not death itself would stop him.

He was a charming, handsome guy with a rapier wit and taste for all things fabulous. So smartly dressed and polite, that's what I remember. One of a kind, as they say. But the one characteristic that sticks in my mind about George was that he did things. He made things happen. His thoughts became things, which is a philosophy I use to this day.

Michael Cepress, photo by Curtis Bryant, New York City

Michael Cepress
Artist, Designer, Curator

I was born about fourteen months before Hibiscus left this earth, and have navigated my first thirty-some years as an artist, clothing maker and culture-lover. I had the great pleasure of passing through school systems, and the even more seducing School of Real Life to guide me toward the faces of icons, idols, creative brothers and sisters who hold a match that constantly re-lights my creative flame. In the midst of a modern existence that doesn't leave much room for artists, eccentrics and those dwelling outside the box, that candle flame can flicker. Those heroic faces become not mere inspiration, but stack up to become the stones of a foundation anchored in support of a creative culture meant to continue for centuries.

Learning the rich life story of Hibiscus through the voices of family, friends, and creative partners was like meeting a kindred soul who could see inside my mind and know where my heart lies. Photographs and film of this magical man are a lesson in what true freedom and artistic liberation looks like. Traces of the past and glimpses of the future are told though his three-dimensional visions on stage and in a vibrant daily life. Hibiscus has shown me that our dreams need not only exist in our minds but can move to our sketchbooks, wardrobes, the songs we sing and the pictures we paint. While I never had the gift of meeting him in this lifetime, it is clear to me that his every step on earth was an homage to the richness of life - where all places, all peoples, all histories are one, and the tools of self-realization are forever within reach.

Hibiscus knew where he came from and where he was going. They say there is nothing new under the sun, and the great blessing of history is that we all stand on the shoulders of those that came before us. If we are lucky we will give voice to whatever may come next. Hibiscus found a particularly bright ray of that sun to stand under, letting his eccentric and radiant voice echo through the boundaries of time and far beyond the temporal barriers of life and death.

Timothy Bellavia
New School professor and family friend

"TRANSplant"

Hibiscus is to some a flower or to others an overpriced bottled flavored iced tea. To me and other performance artists Hibiscus is a cultural force who, in his short life, transfixed and influenced audiences from San Francisco and all of Manhattan's then booming glam era art and rock scene.

Hibiscus is the underground darling I wish I would have met. Yet I know so many people that worked with him. As fate would have it I have performed on stage, collaborated with Hibiscus' peers and even lectured to his family members at the university level. That said, I'm beyond grateful that my nearly 25-year tenure in New York has brought the likes of his unconventional family to grace my life.

Hibiscus, like many New Yorkers, is a transplant, uprooted by his family's common desire to act, perform and create art in a hopeful place – Manhattan's (Lower East Side). My many talks with his siblings – The Screaming Violets – have afforded me the unique opportunity to hold onto something from the past that I could have never known personally in my own coming of age story. Hibiscus is not the cliché of the disenfranchised gay-soul-gone-to-New-York-to-find-art, liberation and hope in a walk up tenement – he had the utmost support of his family. There wasn't ever that moment when the going was tough and Hibiscus had to reach very far for the eyeliner. His sisters and brothers brought the eyeliner to him and forever had his back.

My favorite Hibiscus story is when his sister Eloise shared with me that when his actress mother Ann Harris would put young Hibiscus to bed there were remnants of glitter on him or near him where he lay. Coincidence is G*d's way of remaining anonymous. Hibiscus was born that way and instead of his family redirecting him like most G*d fearing morons would do -they just added stage lights and feathers.

Hibiscus in Manhattan to me represents hope. Manhattan is now hopeless. Sadly, not much glitter is left. In Hibiscus' time and some time after his passing the streets of downtown Manhattan were full of artisans with thrift store finery and trans-glam couture. Today downtown gives way to folks with large Swiss bank accounts; nannies and folks that actually pay retail for their clothes. Hibiscus was a pied piper and predated Marlo Thomas in her Free to Be … You and Me philosophy to the then hip youngsters of the 1970s that embraced their own uniqueness.

Change is inevitable and nothing lasts forever. Our youth fades as does our glitter. Hibiscus represents a time that was part divine, decadent and indeed quite free. Yet something always remains. Because of Hibiscus I can enter a room wearing eyeliner with dignity.

Kenneth Ansloan
(aka Tequila Mockingbyrd)
Head Doll at The Dolls Theater Company,
Albuquerque, New Mexico

HOW HIBISCUS INFLUENCED
MY LIFE

It's funny how sometimes there are memories that are etched in your mind so deeply that you can remember vividly what that day was like. My partner, the late Geneva Convention and I went with a few friends to see *The Cockettes* film documentary. It was fall and the air was crisp and fragrant. We dressed ourselves in high drag in honor of The Cockettes. We painted our faces with our brightest glitter and adorned ourselves in our biggest headdresses. Be damned whoever had to sit behind us in the theater!

The Dolls are a drag performance group that started in Albuquerque, New Mexico in 1997. Matt (aka Geneva Convention) and I always had an obsession with show tunes, fashion and old movies (especially Joan Crawford and Bette Davis and all the other broads who loved suffering on the silver screen in minks). So seeing *The Cockettes* documentary was somewhat of a revelation.

When the lights dimmed and the documentary commenced and the people behind us groaned and moved seats, we knew that magic was in the making. The moment we saw Hibiscus singing in a tree "Can't Help Lovin' Dat Man" we realized here was a twin spirit! A man in drag who loved performing and musicals as much as we did!

For years after, the prospect of writing a play about The Cockettes boiled in the back of my mind like a percolator! But it wasn't until 2007 when my partner Matt was diagnosed with cancer that I started writing a script. We knew that Matt's time was limited. We would always write our scripts together but for this play Matt was just too ill. I think I started writing it as therapy. I remember every night I would read Matt what I had written. I loved the way his eyes shone. It was both beautiful and heartbreaking. Matt died just prior to my completing the play. My memories of that day when we went to see *The Cockettes* documentary were vivid. And something miraculous happened while writing the play. Hibiscus is somewhat of an enigma in the documentary. Yes - he is over the top and outrageous, a mad Nijinsky dancing to his own beat. But he is also mysterious and puzzling at the same time. As I was writing, I felt I got to know Hibiscus. The dialogue flowed. Even though I never knew him, I feel close to him. He inspires me. His dedication to beauty and art never ceases to rouse me. The play was everything I could have hoped for.

The memory of Hibiscus lives on. Memories of him burn bright. His enduring spirit flourishes rather than diminishes. I think this is because we like to see ourselves in him. Who isn't inspired by someone who is not afraid to live out their dreams no matter how decadent, wild or over the top they are? I like to think that The Dolls manage to do this. Long live glitter, fairy dust and show tunes!!!

The last word …. Rumi Missabu and Geretta [from the Michael Varrati Interview with Rumi and Geretta, conclusion]

Final question for you both: What would you want people to know about Hibiscus?

> **Geretta:** He was just amazing! He was cute, funny, talented, and had a wicked sense of humor. He was the nicest person ever. Off-stage, he was more George than Hibiscus, if that makes sense. In his way, he was like Fred from The B-52s mixed with David Lynch, he had this twisted San Fran artistic esthetic. If you add sequins to that, plus a strong sense of family, that was him. Also, boy, did he have an eye for talent.

> **Rumi:** I would want people to know how important he was and how revolutionary he was, not just in regard to the sexual revolution, but in theater. His work was groundbreaking and new. It's incredible how important his work became. We didn't know that at the time, of course, but the legacy this has created has been amazing. I still never know what's around the corner

because of the opportunities that we created all that time ago. It's just amazing, and I want to make sure that Hibiscus is recognized as a free spirit in gay liberation. (4)

George Harris III aka Hibiscus de la Blossom
September 6, 1949 – May 6, 1982

Meet the Authors

(L to R)
Jayne Anne Harris,
Mary Lou Harris
and Eloise Harris

Photo by
Michael Ian

Hibiscus' sisters, Jayne Anne, Eloise and Mary Lou Harris, were very young when the famous "Flower Power" photo was taken. They recall many conversations about the significance and impact that Bernie Boston's image of their brother had on the turbulent and violent issues in the world at that time.

The Harris Sisters were born "in a trunk" as they say in show business. Spending a lifetime in theater, music, art and now publishing, they are eyewitnesses to many of the great artistic revolutions, movements, revolutionaries and pioneers of the 20th century.

Raised within the theatrical and LGBTQ communities of New York City, they have learned first hand that there are magical, magnetic people in this world who leave an indelible mark on those they meet. People who make you feel part of something special. Who make you laugh, dance and love the life you're living just because they lead the way with joy, love and curiosity. Jayne Anne, Eloise and Mary Lou thank their brother Hibiscus for being one of those magical people, and cheering them on as they stumbled through life. Hibiscus gave his family the key to unlock the door to the adventures of a lifetime.

Jayne Anne, Eloise and Mary Lou live in Manhattan and upstate New York. Read the Harris Family's full story in their memoir, *Caravan to Oz: a family reinvents itself off-off Broadway*. www.caravantooz.com

227

In Memoriam

Ann Marie McCanless Harris
(1926-2016)

by Walter Michael Harris

Photo by Charles Caron (circa 1970)

We celebrate our fabulous mother Ann Harris who left this world on September 10, 2016, after a life filled with music, adventure and motherhood. She was a supremely talented actress, dancer, playwright and songwriter. Her father was Fred McCanless, a successful Westchester dentist. Her mother, Anne Marie Driscoll, was musical, creative and the fiery daughter of Jim "Sol D" Driscoll, an Irish immigrant who distinguished himself in the St. Lawrence Seaway lumber business. She and her first son, George III (aka Hibiscus) started a children's theater company in the family's Florida garage in the early 1960s. All the siblings – Walter Michael, Frederic, Jayne Anne, Eloise and Mary Lou – joined in the fun. Inspired by the results, the whole family moved to New York City and began a successful career in show business.

Ann wrote music and lyrics for the off-Broadway productions *Sky High, Speakeasy, Enchanted Miracle* and *Hibiscus.* She has written songs for many other Harris family and Angels of Light shows including *Bluebeard, The Sheep and the Cheapskate, MacBee, There Is Method In Their Madness, Birdie Follies, Gossamer Wings, Razzamatazz, Sky High (the revival), Tinsel Town Tirade* and

Dear Friends of Allegro Sanitation. She performed in and/or choreographed dance numbers in most of them and collaborated with Hibiscus as songwriter and creative consultant. With her son Fred she co-wrote songs for *Hibiscus and the Screaming Violets'* art-rock show.

Her children's musical, *Bluebeard,* has played from coast to coast. She toured Europe with The Angels of Light and has appeared at La MaMa ETC, Judson Poets Theater, Theater for the New City, the New York Shakespeare Festival Public Theater, Caffe Cino, at Lincoln Center and in summer stock.

Ann originated the role of Martha Truitt in the world premiere of Lanford Wilson's *The Rimers of Eldritch* at La MaMa ETC in New York, directed by the playwright. She has a growing fan base for her role as Doris Acker in the cult film classic, *The Honeymoon Killers,* often broadcast around Halloween on Turner Classic Movies.

She was a favorite actress of the late, great off-off-Broadway playwright H.M. Koutoukas and was directed by him in several of his plays. Ann, her children and her husband George are considered pioneers in off-off-Broadway theater and performance art.

Ann – somewhere you are teaching the angels to tap.

George Edgerly Harris II,
aka George, Sr., (1921-2005)

George was born in Bronxville, New York, to Ruth Hoffman Colony and George Edgerly Harris (the first), both artists. His paternal grandfather was Charles Xavier Harris, a successful fine art painter, art professor and expert on the artists of New Amsterdam (early New York City). George's mother, Ruth "Ruthie" Coloney SoRelle, was a talented photographer and a freelance journalist. His late sister, Susan Joyce Harris Weimer, is a fine art painter and retired educator.

George Sr. attended school in Margaretville and Scarsdale, NY, and served in the Air Force as a radio trainer during World War Two. He played drums through high school in a successful dance band formed with his cousin. After the war George attended Columbia University on the GI Bill. In 1948 he married Ann Marie McCanless of Bronxville, where the first four of their six children were born. His days in Florida and subsequent theater journey are detailed in this book.

As an actor and director George was a regular in the experimental off-off-Broadway movement, often performing with Ann and in Hibiscus' shows. In 1968 he made his Broadway debut in *The Great White Hope* along with James Earl Jones and Jane Alexander. He worked steadily in movies, including *Superman,* on television and radio, in summer stock, and national tours. During his career he worked with pioneering producers and playwrights including Ellen Stewart, Joe Cino, Crystal Field and George Bartnieff, Al Carmines and Lanford Wilson; and with renowned actors Henry Fonda, Anne Meara, Billy D. Williams,

230

Gene Wilder, Fred Astaire, Richard Pryor and Frank Sinatra.

He was generous in sharing his experience and expertise with his fellow actors. Norman Thomas, who co-starred with George in *Gorilla Queen*, testifies: "*Gorilla Queen* was my first show. Ever. Anywhere. I had never been in a play, never auditioned, never taken an acting class. My usual, thorough reading of the Village Voice turned up a small classified ad for the casting call at Judson. On a lark, I attended the audition. I had no notion of what I was letting myself in for. Your father took this raggedy-assed hick, just off the bus with the horse shit still on his shoes, from the tomato fields of Hanover County, Virginia under his wing and eased the transition from rube to avant-garde actor. His kindness made a wonderful difference to my life and career."

A lifelong musician and lover of big band music, George became a successful and respected bandleader in his own right during the 1970s, in New York City, where his Ninth Street Stompers were a popular act. The band featured many A-list musicians and launched or revived their careers. George worked on staff for the Musician's Union Local 802 in New York until his retirement. He was proud of his service during World War II and participated in the Memorial Day parade each year in Margaretville, NY, the town where he was born and where every day of his retirement was a new adventure.

Dad passed away December 5, 2005. His proudest achievement was his family.

L to R: George Harris Sr., Christopher Reeve and David Baxt in the 1978 movie Superman. *Photo © Warner Brothers, courtesy CapedWonder.com*

A word of thanks

Writing a memoir is like opening a *matryoshka,* (Russian nesting doll) – people within people within people, and every one a complete life story. Every new answer conceals a dozen new questions. While it's fun to play Sherlock Holmes and find clues that reveal the connections, the search would be difficult without the help of our extended family members, living and past, who helped fill in the blanks.

Thanks to our fabulous contributors, photographers, co-performers and collaborators that "nest" within our story. Thanks also to those who read our rough manuscripts and offered their invaluable wisdom and expertise: James D. Gossage, Susan Dale Rose, Patricia Mansfield Harris, Robert Croonquist and Jim Pietsch. We thank Becky Simmons, Archivist for the Bernie Boston Collection, RIT Archive Collections, for her support; Jodi Steele for designing our cover, David Belisle for photo restoration, Jim Pietsch for media support and Magie Dominic and Andrea Simmons for their advice and enthusiasm.

And big thanks to our tireless editor, contributor, collaborator and brother, Walter Michael Harris, whose work shines on every page.

A big writing project like this requires time away from our families, so we thank them for their understanding and patience: Jim Pietsch, Miles V. Pietsch, Thomas Kelley, Quinn Kelley, Joe Damone, Montana Damone, Patricia Mansfield Harris, Kristin Green, Chad Syme, Avonlea Green, Juniper Green, Jason Green, Irish Benito Green, Joshua Green, and Jamie Green.

Thanks to all the producers, writers and artists, champions of creativity and freedom, who supported and inspired our brother and family along the way, including John Mayo, Ellen Stewart, Joe Cino, Al Carmines, Robert Patrick, David Hockney, Michael Butler, Crystal Field, George Bartinieff, Alex Bartenieff, Ritsaert ten Cate, Louis Friedman, Bill Weber and David Weissman.

Finally, the *Flower Power Man* team thanks you, the reader, for taking an interest in our brother's story. We hope you enjoyed it and will tell others about it. The world needs flower power now more than ever.

232

Thank you to our amazing contributors!
(in alphabetical order)

Robert Altman is an American photographer. After graduation from Hunter College in New York, Altman was taught photography by Ansel Adams. Following his early success as chief staff photographer for Rolling Stone he expanded into fashion photography and fine art. For a decade beginning in the mid 90s Altman taught web design and Photoshop as adjunct professor for several institutions including San Francisco State University and the University of California, Berkeley. In May 2010, he was presented with a Doctor of Arts, *Honoris Causa*, from Digital Media Arts College. Altman has exhibited at Abbey Road Studios in London, The Beat Museum in San Francisco, Bethel Woods Center for the Arts, the Newseum in New York City, the Georgia Historical Society. Altman has been published in dozens of books, magazines and newspapers and his work is a part of the permanent collections of The San Francisco Public Library, The Library of Congress in Washington DC, The Smithsonian Institution, The Rock and Roll Hall of Fame, and the Kodak Rock Photography Collection.

Kenneth Ansloan is a writer, actor and the creator and driving force behind The Dolls theater troupe of Albuquerque, NM. Kenneth writes, produces and acts in as many as four original shows a year. He has written Drag Westerns, Sci-Fi Adventures, a Fairy-Tale series and several annual Christmas Holiday Spectaculars. All are outrageous fun with a track record for entertaining audiences and creating a growing fan base. His 2015 play, *Angels of Light, the story of the Cockettes,* takes a psychedelic trip to the 60's. It's a tale about The Cockettes, San Francisco's infamous gender-bending drag troupe, as they soar to dizzying heights of fame only to sink to the very depths of despair. For a profile of Ken, visit http://www.abqjournal.com/703645/the-8.html

Penny Arcade has garnered countless fans worldwide with an emotionally and intellectually charged performance style. Internationally revered as writer, director and actress, she has influenced generations of artists around the world. While Penny Arcade is considered the Queen of Underground Performance she has had a mainstream presence outside of America since 1993 and her work has been produced everywhere from Calgary to Sydney, London Vienna, Rio, Zagreb, Zurich, Belfast, Oslo, Lisbon, Mexico City, Glasgow, Dublin and Vancouver but her larger full length work has not been produced in the USA outside of NY, LA and SF. http://pennyarcade.tv/

Timothy Bellavia is an award-winning children's author, illustrator and educator. He is an alumnus of Skowhegan School of Painting and Sculpture. Bellavia's art has hung in museums and galleries around the world. Mr. Bellavia has also worked as an independent curator at the Lower East Side Tenement Museum, has appeared on the runways of several alternative fashion shows and has danced back-up for the pop star Cyndi Lauper. Mr. Bellavia recently presented his doll-making curriculum on the International Day of Tolerance at the United Nations. The New York City Department of Education realized the value of the curriculum and awarded Mr. Bellavia's T.I.M.M.E. Company a contract. This contract has allowed Bellavia to amplify the company's mission to teach tolerance to New York City's school children while integrating the arts into the literacy curriculum. He currently teaches in the School of Education & Psychology, Graduate Division at Touro College, in New York City. http://www.timothydbellavia.com/

Andrew Blauvelt is Curator of Architecture and Design and Chief of Communications and Audience Engagement at the Walker Art Center in Minneapolis. A practicing graphic designer, his work has received numerous awards and has been published and exhibited in North America, Europe, and Asia. He has organized numerous exhibitions. https://en.wikipedia.org/wiki/Andrew_Blauvelt

234

Bernie Boston (May 18, 1933 – January 22, 2008) was a celebrated American photographer most noted for his iconic _Flower Power_ image. An archive of many of Boston's negatives, prints and contact sheets is held at the Rochester Institute of Technology today. Established as a tribute to his memory and a lasting inspiration for young photographers, it includes most of his work including the original negative for "Flower Power" For more, visit the RIT Archive: http://library.rit.edu/findingaids/html/RITArc.0416.html#colloverview

Michael Cepress is an American Artist, Curator, and Educator. A deep passion for the cultural impact clothing and fashion can make has led Cepress to focus on the design of his own fashion label and costumes for theatre and stage performance. Cepress has exhibited and lectured nationally and internationally as an authority on the historical importance of fashion as art. In 2015, he became Guest Curator at the Bellevue Arts Museum, and debuted a 9000-square-foot exhibition titled _Counter-Couture,_ featuring over 150 authentic garments from the American counterculture of the 1960s and 1970s. In 2017 _Counter-Couture_ was showcased at the Museum of Arts and Design in New York City. He has dressed the Seattle Symphony Orchestra for their Carnegie Hall performances and designed for legendary theatre director Robert Wilson. His work has been published in The New York Times, VOGUE, NY Magazine, The New Yorker, Women's Wear Daily, Huffington Post, OUT Magazine, Surface Design Journal, and a host of books. An Instructor in the University of Washington's School of Art for 11 years, he has created curriculum on multiple facets of Fashion Design, Wearable Art, and the history of style and clothing. In Summer 2016 Cepress was a guest instructor at the Penland School of Crafts, and in May 2016 was inducted into the Hall of Fame in his hometown of Wausau, Wisconsin.

Robert Croonquist was a college student when he came up to San Francisco from the Peninsula to see The Cockettes in the streets and onstage and thought they were the bravest people he had ever seen in his life. He was a big fan of the San Francisco Angels of Light, their

Photo by Lauren

philosophy of Free and worked with Tahara and Tree in transforming the Kaliflower Commune's Shotwell Street yard from asphalt to garden. In the mid Seventies he lived communally at 529 Castro Street on the block with Harvey Milk's Camera Shop and The Hula Palace where his household collectively created feminist, anti-imperialist street theater and were a pro-feminist male delegation to the UN's first International Year of the Woman conference in Mexico City in 1975. He co-founded the Office for Political Prisoners and Human Rights in Chile and Gay Solidarity with the Chilean Resistance. He lived for six years in a digger commune in the mountains of eastern Mendocino County and is on the Board of Directors of the San Francisco-based Life Frames, Inc. In New York he worked crew with Theater for the New City's annual Street Theater and continues to collaborate there, bringing neighboring high school students and atomic bomb survivors from Hiroshima and Nagasaki together for daylong theater workshops with Hibakusha Stories, an oral history and disarmament education initiative of the UN NGO he founded in 2005, Youth Arts New York.

Laurence Frommer is a graduate of New York University's Tisch School of the Arts. His New York credits include Angry Hotzmach in the Yiddish musical, *The Witch* (Ben Zemach, NYU), Aegithus in *Electra (*Playwrights Horizons, NYU), Harry Ritz as Hermann Goering in the musical, *I and I* (Living Theater), Yankel in the musical, *Garment for the Moon* (Westbeth), Mona in *Fortune in Men's Eyes* (Matamashita Theater), Buzzlebub in an American Premiere of Lully's Opera, *Amadis*, and Tuzenbach in *The Three Sisters* (Michael Parva, dir.). Laurence is a part of a cabaret act with Ray Hagan who friends of La Mama remember as the Stripping Nun in Julie Bovasso's *Gloria and Esperanza*.

William Frothingham, aka Palm Spareengz, worked for over thirty - five years in the flower and interior design businesses. While still a teenager, he was involved with Ze Whiz Kidz theatre for a few years from its beginning. He remains grateful to this day for those

236

experiences and those people who became his friends, mentors and guides. Based in Seattle, William continues as a design collector and consultant under the scrutiny of his faithful Abyssinian cat, Sascha.

Laurence Gartel began creating digital art long before the birth of the personal computer and is considered the father of the genre. His 40-year career started working alongside video guru Nam June Paik at Media Study/Buffalo in upstate New York. Growing up in New York City during the Punk Rock era he was friends with Stiv Bators, Sid Vicious, Joey Ramone and Wendy O. Williams, and exhibited his work with Robert Mapplethorpe. He taught Andy Warhol how to use the Amiga computer in order to produce the album cover for Debbie Harry (Blondie). His work has been exhibited by the Museum of Modern Art, Long Beach Museum of Art, Princeton Art Museum, Norton Museum of Art as well as in permanent collections of the Smithsonian Institution's Museum of American History, Bibliothèque nationale de France at Paris and the Victoria and Albert Museum, London. Mr. Gartel has traveled the world exhibiting and projecting his work in Australia, Spain, Germany and Italy, as well as India, creating a Bollywood Music/Video for Universal Entertainment. Commissions include artwork for Britney Spears, Justin Timberlake, Red Hot Chili Peppers, as well as for corporations such as Coca Cola, Philip Morris, Walt Disney, National Basketball Association, Gibson Guitars, Bang & Olufsen, and is known to most for his ABSOLUT GARTEL ad for Absolut Vodka. Visit Laurence at www.gartelart.com

James D. Gossage, Photographer. I was introduced to Joe Cino and his Caffe Cino by Robert Berger in 1964, and worked with Berger on several creative projects over the next few years. In 1965, Harry Koutoukas asked me to photograph a benefit for the post fire Caffe Cino at the Writers Stage on East 4th Street. From there, I was invited to Cafe La MaMa at 122 Second Avenue, photographing several of Tom Eyen's productions and producing flyers and posters for his shows. At La MaMa I photographed a rehearsal of George Harris III and his siblings in a production by their 'El Dorado Players'. In the following years I photographed productions of other authors and in other venues including Playbox and Playwrights Workshop. In the 1980s I began creating a comprehensive index of my Off-Off-Broadway photos and several years later completed a database and report structure I was proud of, with resulting cross-reference style reports currently available in 'Google Docs'.

Walter Michael Harris, editor and collaborator, has been around long enough to remember the days before his family "ran away with the circus" of show business. Mr. Harris is retired from a long career in show business. In 1968 he was the youngest member of the original Broadway cast of *Hair*. After relocating to Seattle in 1979 be became a company member of The Group, Seattle's multicultural theater; co-founded Pilgrim Center for the Arts, and was the producing artistic director for ArtsWest Playhouse for five seasons. WMH lives in Seattle with his wife, Patricia Mansfield Harris. He is a proud stepfather of two and grandfather of four.

Fayette Hauser graduated from Boston University, College of Fine Arts with a BFA in painting. After a year in Manhattan, Fayette moved to San Francisco in 1968 where she co-founded the avant-garde experimental theatre group The Cockettes. She performed, designed costumes and extensively photographed the troupe. When The Cockettes disbanded in 1972, Fayette and other members of the group moved to Lower Manhattan to continue performing in underground theater, playing in venues like Caffe Cino, CBGB's, The Bouwerie Lane Theatre and Club 82. In 1975 Fayette moved to Los Angeles to write for CBS and, while there, became a professional photographer. She designed album covers and photographed many of the creative artists in the fertile music scene of Los Angeles in the 70's and 80's. Along with her photography Fayette created a small design business called Atelier Fayette, which featured Wearable Art, one-of-a-kind decorated vests. She sold to many artists such as The Rolling Stones, New Kids On The Block, Arsenio Hall and Diana Ross. In the early 90's Fayette was the costume designer on four feature films and two stage plays for the Strasberg Institute and received two Dramalogue Awards. Fayette's photography has been featured in galleries and museums including the exhibit *West of Center: Art and*

The Counter-Culture Experiment in America, 1965-1977, first
presented by the Denver Museum of Contemporary Art; and *Counter-
Couture: Fashioning Identity in the American Counter-Culture* at the
Bellevue (Washington) Arts Museum, curated by fashion designer
Michael Cepress. www.fayettehauser.com

Robert Heide and John Gilman

Robert: I first met John Gilman through Joe Cino at Mother Hubbard's
Pie and Hamburger Restaurant in Sheridan Square in The Village. My
play *The Bed* was having a good run at Joe's Caffe Cino on Cornelia
Street. This was in 1965; and following that I wrote *Moon* a play about
a young hippie couple who are paid a visit by a violent desperate
menacing couple. After they leave another character, a Parsifal figure,
enters. He is a painter who has just moved in upstairs and brings
freshly baked bread as a neighborly gesture. He paints moons and
other planets in bright, day-glow colors, a contrast to his all white
clothing and his serene demeanor. I directed the play myself and cast
John as Christopher, the artist and he played the part to perfection. We
became fast friends and he went on to play opposite Linda Eskenas in
At War With the Mongols an anti-Vietnam war play I wrote. My other
plays followed in other venues like La MaMa *(Why Tuesday Never
Has a Blue Monday)* and the Manhattan Theater Club. Full length
plays *(Suburban Tremens)* at Westbeth Theater and *Tropical Fever in
Key West* and *Crisis of Identity* at the Theater for the New City all
starred the Village Voice Obie winning actress Regina David.

A new book entitled *Robert Heide - 25 Plays* has been published by
Michael Smith, the chief theater critic in the 60s and 70s at the Village
Voice and now editor and publisher of Fast Books Press, Inc. On the
cover a blurb declares "Including the Caffe Cino Classics *The Bed* and
Moon plus the scenario for Andy Warhol's film *Lupe* starring girl-of-
the year (1966) Edie Sedgwick." The book is available at
fastbookspress.com and on Amazon.

John and I have lived on Christopher Street since the turbulent 60s
days, where we collected Pop-Americana cultural artifacts such as
original litho-on-tin Coca Cola signs, vintage Mickey Mouse cookie
jars, cobalt blue-mirrored Art Deco coffee tables, Depression ware and

colorful Mexicana Fiesta kitchen dishware. All of this led to over a dozen illustrated coffee table books telling the story of America's recent past, including *Popular Art Deco* and *Box Office Buckaroos* (both Abbeville Press), *Home Front America* (Chronicle Books), *Disneyana* (Hyperion), *The Mickey Mouse Watch - From the Beginning of Time* and *Mickey Mouse - The Evolution, the Legend, The Phenomenon!* both from Disney Editions, *Starstruck, Dimestore Dream Parade* and many others from publishers like E. P. Dutton, Doubleday, and St. Martin's Press. Read more about our adventures and books and plays at robertheideandjohngilman.blogspot.com where you can watch a PowerPoint illustrated lecture at the New School featuring Robert talking about Andy Warhol in Greenwich Village.

John Edward Heys is an American independent filmmaker, actor and writer who lives and works in Berlin. After two semesters of college majoring in Liberal Arts, Heys moved to New York City in 1968 and became part of the East Village and West Village alternative life and LGBTQ culture. In August 1969, he founded America's first bi-monthly newspaper for the LGBTQ community, *Gay Power*, the official title totaling 24 issues, and was its editor until August 1970. One of its covers was created by Robert Mapplethorpe. The newspaper also contained illustrations by Touko Laaksonen, better known as Tom of Finland, as well as regular contributions from thought leaders and organizations throughout the LGBTQ universe. Heys created several one-man performance pieces and he acted with Cookie Mueller, H.M. Koutoukas, Charles Ludlam, Ethyl Eichleberger and as part of The Angels of Light NYC group which Hibiscus founded after moving back to New York City. Heys was the subject for the artists Peter Hujar, Francesco Clemente, Charles Ludlam, Richard Banks, Frank Moore and numerous other photographers. Heys was a close friend and muse of the photographer Peter Hujar and subject of many portraits. Heys' films have been screened at many worldwide film festivals. https://en.wikipedia.org/wiki/John_Edward_Heys

David Loehr grew up on a farm in Western Massachusetts, studied graphic design at Parson's School of Design in New York and attended the Lester Polokov School for Stage Design. In 1974 a friend gave him the book, *James Dean: The Mutant King* by David Dalton. David read the book while travelling from New York to California.

240

While in California, he saw all three of Dean's major films on the big screen for the first time, and was knocked out by Dean's performances. In 1988, David opened the James Dean Gallery to the public for the first time. David has worked on dozens of James Dean projects including books, documentaries and numerous television shows, both national and local including: A Current Affair, 20/20, To Tell the Truth, Entertainment Tonight, The Joe Franklin Show, New York Profiles, Across Indiana, Strange Universe, The Good Night Show, and a live, in studio appearance on a popular Japanese television show. David currently publishes a quarterly James Dean Gallery Newsletter and continues to operate the Museum Exhibit and Gift Shop in Fairmount. http://jamesdeangallery.com/david.html

Dagmar Krajnc is a photographer/writer whose work is published in many international magazines and books on *HAIR* (the musical, for which she was the official photographer), Elvis Presley, David Bowie, Eric Clapton, Elton John, Rod Stewart, Donna Summer, Faces and The Rolling Stones. Visit Dagmar at http://dagmarfotos.com/

Lance Loud was a bold pioneer of gay awareness who exited the closet on national television in 1973 on the pre-reality television sensation *An American Family*, journalist and occasional actor. Lance Loud was a frequent contributor to The Advocate in addition to appearing in such films as 1981's *Subway Riders* and 1993's *Inside Monkey Zetterland*. http://www.pbs.org/lanceloud/

Kembrew McLeod is a Professor of Communication Studies at the University. He has published and produced several books and documentaries about music and popular culture, and his writing has appeared in the New York Times, Slate, and Rolling Stone. Kembrew's book Freedom of Expression® received an American Library Association book award, and his most recent documentary, *Copyright Criminals*, aired on PBS's Emmy Award-winning documentary series, *Independent Lens*. His first documentary, *Money For Nothing*, was programmed at the

2002 South by Southwest Film Festival and the 2002 New England Film and Video Festival, where it received the Rosa Luxemburg Award for Social Consciousness. McLeod's second documentary, *Freedom of Expression®: Resistance and Repression in the Age of Intellectual Property*, was distributed by the Media Education Foundation—*Freedom of Expression®* serves as a companion to his book of the same name, which won the American Library Association's Oboler book award for "best scholarship in the area of intellectual freedom" in 2006. McLeod co-authored the book *Creative License: The Law and Culture of Digital Sampling* and the anthology *Cutting Across Media: Appropriation Art, Interventionist Collage and Copyright Law*, both published by Duke University Press in 2011. Most recently, New York University Press published his book *Pranksters: Making Mischief in the Modern World* on April 1, 2014. McLeod's music and cultural criticism have appeared in *Rolling Stone, SPIN, Slate, MOJO, New York Times, Los Angeles Times, Washington Post, Village Voice*, and *The New Rolling Stone Album Guide*.

Agosto Machado is an actor, known for *Beautiful Darling*, 2010; *Keep the Lights On*, 2012; and *Jack Smith and the Destruction of Atlantis*, 2006; the documentaries *Untitled David France Project, 2012*; *Pay It No Mind: Marsha P. Johnson*, 2012; *Superstar in a Housedress*, 1973; the short subjects *In Search of Avery Willard*, 2012; *Minette: Portrait of a Part-Time Lady*, 2006; and the reality TV series *An American Family*, Episode #1.2,1973. Agosto is a long-time close friend of Ann Harris and her family. For more, visit: http://www.imdb.com/name/nm1542652/

HRH Lee Mentley began wearing poodle skirts at age 4. Lee was raised by a honky-tonk mom straight out of *Pink Flamingo*s, ran through the streets of East LA in day-glow hair in the 1960s, graduated from University of California at Long Beach where he helped create the very first gay student union in California, and after being invited by The Cockettes in Greenwich Village in 1971, moved to San Francisco where many of his royal adventures take place. His new book, *The Princess of Castro Street*, recounts his life in San Francisco. For more, visit: hrhleementley.com

Adrian Milton is one of those rare individuals who seems almost magically to be at the center of history in the making. Driven by an insatiable curiosity and a love of visual beauty and intellectual stimulation, he has traveled far and wide to see, partake and create. The result is a life that reads like an adventure novel and a body of work rich in layers of sources and meaning. He struck out for New York City as soon as he had graduated from high school. Arriving in 1959 at the age of 17, he immediately found the playground he always yearned for. Studying Art History at Columbia University opened up the rich visual pageant of past centuries. Thus began a career in painting, performance, writing, film and other media, always with a knack for predicting the future zeitgeist.
http://adrianmiltonart.com

Rumi Missabu, aka James Bartlett, is an actor director producer mentor archivist and original Cockette. Career highlights include *Elevator Girls In Bondage, The Cockettes, Thrillpeddlers, Pearls Over Shanghai, The Cockettes in Paris, The Crystal Ball, Keeping The Tigers Away, Uncle Bob, The Questioning of John Rykener,* and *Ruminations.* The James Bartlett (Rumi Missabu) Papers, a queer archive of original memorabilia, ephemera and personal papers resides in the New York Public Library for the Performing Arts at Lincoln Center. His feature-length film *RUMINATIONS* is currently in production from NuReality Productions. For more information, visit www.facebook.com/ruminationsmovie/

Michael Musto - is an American actor, journalist and a former columnist for The Village Voice, where he wrote "La Dolce Musto." He is the author of *Downtown* and *Manhattan on the Rocks* as well as a compilation of selected columns published as *La Dolce Musto.*
https://en.wikipedia.org/wiki/Michael_Musto

Dan Nicoletta is a freelance photographer with a passion for portraiture and the way people express themselves. Over the past 35 years Dan has developed great working relationships with colleagues in countless areas of expertise and a love for working with people, especially artists working in film and theatre. Dan has 35 years of stock photography available on a wide variety of subjects with a strong emphasis on gay, lesbian, bisexual, & transgender culture. LGBT San Francisco: The Daniel Nicoletta Photographs, Chronicles his years at the center of the gay liberation movement, Reel Art Press, 2017 http://www.dannynicoletta.com/

Bobby Reed is a lifer. From Middletown, New York to Off-Broadway to Hollywood, he's still at it, in a performing and producing career that spans over 50 years. While beginning on the stage at six years old (*Hansel & Gretel*), he's moved into film and television, and of course, the Web. 75+ plays, 100+ films, multiple television appearances and 35 web series and pilots, Bobby keeps cranking out the creative product, year after year. He's also a well-known marketing coach, teaching his popular *SuperMarketing for Actors* around Hollywood and New York, trying to teach performers that the only thing that counts in show business is longevity. His many clips and scenes (as well as the whole, long story) are on bobbyreed.com. Enjoy.

Tim Robbins is an Academy Award-winning actor, director, screenwriter, producer, musician and activist. His extensive career and many awards can be found online. He is also a father and humanitarian. Tim founded and directs The Actor's Gang, an experimental theater company based in Los Angeles. http://www.theactorsgang.com

Susan Dale Rose is a writer, horsewoman and professionally curious human being. She lives in her beloved New Mexico with husband, daughters, granddaughter, horses, dogs and cats and an assortment of wildlife. She looked up to Hibiscus -- then George -- as the eldest cousin, and didn't know how to fill those shoes when he died. She is the author of Way Beyond Pisgah, What Horses Have Taught Me and Upon our Westward Way, with two other books in final review.

Denise Ryan is an award-winning feature writer with the Vancouver Sun. She lives in Vancouver, Canada.

244

Lendon Sadler was born in Atlanta, Georgia in 1950 and was inspired as a young teen by the peace movement and Martin Luther King, Jr., whom he knew from his neighborhood. "Besides the hippies," he told me, "the Civil Rights organizers were the most inspirational movement at the time because they had so much energy." He eventually ran away from home, traversing the 1960s on a long, strange bohemian trip that eventually took him to the West Coast. "Flying into San Francisco for the first time in my life, I felt settled. Even before I got out of the plane, just seeing the Pacific Ocean was incredible."
http://littlevillagemag.com/prairie-pop-flashback-to-70s-sanfran-drag-with-former-cockette-lendon-sadler/

Ilka Scobie is a native New Yorker who teaches poetry in the city school system. She writes about contemporary art for London Artlyst and Brooklyn Rail. Recent poetry has appeared in Urban Graffitti, here/there, and the anthology Resist Much/Obey Little. She is a deputy editor of Live Mag.

Andrew Sherwood was an "early adopter" of the Harris Family when we arrived in New York City from Florida, Andrew became the Harris Family piano and voice teacher, family photographer and loyal friend. Thanks to his artistry and skill we always had the best promotional and show photos in town. Andrew is now living in Paris, visits when he can and remains in close touch.

Jodi Steele designed our book's dynamic cover. With a growing portfolio of creative projects, Jodi took on designing the Harris family books and websites with typical enthusiasm. While she calls the Pacific Northwest home, Jodi is passionate about supporting and fanning the flames of artistic fire everywhere. www.lovesteele.com; @SteeleBeams. Instagram: mixed_metal

David Talbot is an American progressive journalist, author and media entrepreneur. He is the founder and former CEO and editor-in-chief of one of the first web magazines, *Salon*. Talbot founded *Salon* in 1995 when the web was still in its infancy and is considered one of the pioneers of online journalism. Under Talbot's leadership, the magazine gained a large following and broke several major national stories. Since leaving Salon, Talbot has established a reputation as a historian, working on the Kennedy assassination and other areas of "hidden history." Talbot has worked as a senior editor for Mother Jones magazine and a features editor for The San Francisco Examiner, and has written for Time magazine, The New Yorker, Rolling Stone, and other publications. https://en.wikipedia.org/wiki/David_Talbot

Claudia Tedesco Colmer was raised on the Upper West Side of Manhattan. Her father was a television director. From that accident of birth she became interested in theatre first working as an extra age 13 in T.V and film. She met George at 14 and he brought her into the world of off-off Broadway, and later to San Francisco. Claudia performed at the Caffe Cino, Theatre for the New City, and sang in the Milos Forman film "I'm Taking Off." In her twenties she left acting and obtained a Master's degree in Social Work. She married the English visual artist Roy Colmer who died in 2014. His paintings and films will be exhibited in Nov.2017 at the Lisson Gallery in London. Claudia still practices social work, lives and works in Los Angeles.

Pam Tent aka Sweet Pam was a core member of The Cockettes throughout their heyday and she continued to perform onstage at the Palace Theatre with John Waters' stars, Divine and Mink Stole. After moving to NYC she teamed up with several of Ze Seattle Whiz Kidz, Warhol luminaries and other Cockettes where she sang blues at the Palm Casino Revue. While performing at CBGBs she also hooked up with Dee Dee Ramone and the fledgling punk rock scene. The author of *Midnight at the Palace: My Life as a Fabulous Cockette,* Pam has since collaborated and performed with Scrumbly Koldewyn on rewrites of two original Cockette productions, *Tinsel Tarts in a Hot Coma* and *Pearls Over Shanghai* with the Thrillpeddlers in San Francisco's Hypnodrome. https://www.amazon.com/Midnight-Palace-Life-Fabulous-Cockette/dp/B007K5349M

Mark Thompson (author-activist) began his writing career at the national gay and lesbian newsmagazine *The Advocate* in 1975, reporting on culture and politics in Europe. Thompson is best known, however, for his influential trilogy of books dealing with gay spirituality. The first in the series, *Gay Spirit: Myth and Meaning* (Lethe Press) was published in 1987. The anthology has been acclaimed around the world and was recently included on a list

246

compiled by the *Lambda Book Report* of the "100 Lesbian and Gay Books That Changed Our Lives." The Los Angeles Times called *Gay Spirit* an "exciting challenge to conventional thinking."
http://www.markthompsongayspirit.com/

Shelley Valfer began his career in the "professional theater" as the assistant stage manager for the "Angels of Light" show *Gossamer Wings* at Theater for the New City on Jane Street in 1973. He continued working with TNC through 1974 when he traveled with them to Parma, Italy to perform in a show at the International Student Theater Festival there. He stayed in Italy where he met up with Robert Wilson's Byrd Hoffman School of Byrds and became assistant stage manager for their production of *A Letter for Queen Victoria* at the Spoleto Festival. He continued working as an actor and performer with Bob Wilson and other avant-garde companies such as the Bread and Puppet Theater. He was Tour Accountant for the Allman Brothers Band with whom he worked from 1994 until 2014. Since then he has returned to his roots as an actor and has been appearing in various theater, puppetry, film and television projects, most recently as the lead in an episode of "Homicide for the Holidays" on the Oxygen network, playing mass murderer Gene Simmons.
http://www.broadwayworld.com/people/bio/Shelley-Valfer/
http://www.abouttheartists.com/artists/463333-shelley-valfer

Michael Varrati is a screenwriter, actor and pop culture enthusiast. In addition to the Dreams segment of the award-winning anthology *Tales of Poe*, Michael is also the writer behind the horror comedy *The Sins of Dracula*, the sci-fi short *Crash Site*, the Euro-Horror inspired *Flesh for the Inferno*, among others. In addition to his work on the silver screen, Michael's writing has appeared in a number of publications, including *The Huffington Post, NewNowNext, FearNet, Videoscope magazine, VideoInk News, Tubefilter*, and a celebrated regular column on *peacheschrist.com*. Michael is also one of the core members behind the popular exploitation and horror publication Ultra Violent, and was voted by Agents of Geek as one of the "Top People to Follow in 2014." http://www.huffingtonpost.com/author/michael-varrati

Bill Weber, editor/co-director of *The Cockettes* documentary – has been a video editor for over 25 years, editing innovative commercials, music videos, special effects and a variety of long form projects for film and television. His current project as editor is *The Untold Tales of Armisted Maupin,* examining the life and work of one of the world's most beloved storytellers, following his evolution from a conservative son of the Old South into a gay rights pioneer whose novels have inspired millions to claim their own truth.

David Weissman, producer/co-director of *The Cockettes* documentary – is an award winning independent filmmaker whose films have been broadcast domestically and internationally, and have been featured at countless film festivals, including Berlin, Sundance, and Telluride. His current project is *Conversations With Gay Elders,* a series of in-depth interviews focused on gay men whose journeys of self-discovery precede the era of Stonewall and Gay Liberation.

François Weyergans is a Belgian writer and director. François Weyergans was elected to the Académie Française on 26 March 2009. He started film studies at the IDHEC (Hautes Études Cinématographiques), where he came to love the films of Robert Bresson and Jean-Luc Godard. He soon began to write for Cahiers du Cinéma and directed his first film about Maurice Béjart. https://en.wikipedia.org/wiki/Fran%C3%A7ois_Weyergans

James William Windsor, "Tahara," born 12 August 1950, at Pampa, Texas, son of James William Windsor and Betty Jo (Noel). Came to San Francisco, California from Dallas, Texas in July 1969. Arrived on 4th of July. Joined Gay Liberation in Berkeley, California in August 1969. In 1969 saw Hibiscus on streets of Berkeley in his exotic outfits and being inspired began to create my own exotic look. At Gay Lib met a man named John Harrill who had been in 1967 with Hibiscus in a play in New York City called *Gorilla Queen.* There was a character in the play named Tahara Nugi Whitewoman. John said I was more of a Tahara, than a Jimmy. So I changed my name to Tahara and have kept it ever since. I was Hibiscus' best friend, until he moved from San Francisco to New York City in 1972. I was in both the Cockettes and the Angels of Light theater groups. Started another group in 1976 called The Assorted Nuts and directed theater at a mental hospital with the patients as actors. Currently live in San Francisco and married to Arnold Rice. Artist.

Holly Woodlawn was a transgender actress and Warhol superstar who appeared in his movies *Trash* and *Women in Revolt*. Holly's story was immortalized in the first lines of the Lou Reed song "Walk on the Wild Side." The song began: "Holly came from Miami, F - L - A - -- Hitch-hiked her way across the U - S - A - -- Plucked her eyebrows on the way - Shaved her legs and then - he was a she. She says, 'Hey, babe, take a walk on the wild side' ."
https://en.wikipedia.org/wiki/Holly_Woodlawn

Martin Worman was an associate professor of theater at Antioch College in Yellow Springs, Ohio when he died of AIDS in 1993. Dubbed "The Cockette Who Could Read" Worman hid the fact that he had a MFA in theater from the C.W. Post Campus of Long Island University during his first year with the anti-intellectual, street savvy Cockettes. With a Vietnam era general discharge from the Army, he arrived in San Francisco to collaborate with Scrumbly Koldewyn, creating some of the Cockettes' most enduring songs and lyrics, from "Gert's Postcard" to "Love Among the Ruins of Antiquity" for The Cockettes' later shows, *Les Etoile de Minuit* and *Hot Greeks*. With co-founder David Baker he brought the Gay Men's Theater Collective's groundbreaking *Crimes Against Nature* to New York where he resided for 15 years, writing and directing theater and teaching NYU's first gay theater class at Tisch School of the Arts. As Dr. Queen, he mentored the remarkable singer, songwriter and environmentalist Anhoni and drag historian and academic Joe E. Jeffreys. Upon Martin's death his lover Robert Croonquist transcribed 600 pages of 90 hours of interviews Worman conducted with Cockettes, many of whom were dying of AIDS, for his unfinished dissertation *Midnight Masquerade*, a history of The Cockettes, which now resides in the Martin Worman Collection at the New York Library for the Performing Arts at Lincoln Center. He was honored to direct, and write for, the Harris family in *Hibiscus and the Screaming Violets*.

Paul Zone grew up in New York during the 1960s. Turning 13 years old in 1970 he was already attending Rock concerts with his older brothers Miki Zone and Mandy Zone. He photographed concerts by Lou Reed, Iggy & The Stooges, Alice Cooper, Kiss, T. Rex and at the clubs Max's Kansas City, Mercer Arts Center & Club 82 photographing The New York Dolls, Suicide, Wayne County and local underground personalities during the New York "Glam Rock" era. By the mid 1970s he was photographing his friends that were just forming their bands during the transition from Glam Rock to Punk Rock. He is likely the only person that has extensive photographs of Blondie, The Ramones, Suicide, Patti Smith, Johnny Thunders, Richard Hell, Talking Heads, among others on the streets, at parties, inside and outside the clubs, on stage, backstage and in the bathrooms of CBGB & Max's Kansas City years before any of them made their debut recording.

Paul and his two brothers also had a band of their own at that time called The Fast, they released 5 influential singles, 2 LPs and Paul was also the resident DJ upstairs at Max's Kansas City nightly. In the 1980s, Paul and brother Miki, now an Electro duo called Man 2 Man, scored pop hit singles through out Europe, Australia, Mexico, South America & South Africa including "Male Stripper," "Who Knows What Evil?," "Energy Is Eurobeat" & "I Need A Man." Paul Zone's photography has been exhibited in Berlin, Rome, Barcelona, Amsterdam, Canada and throughout America. His new book, "Playground: Growing Up In The New York Underground" (Glitterati Inc.) released in 2015 is a pictorial & biographical memoir of his life through the 1970s and 1980s.

Quote and Photo Credits

Thanks to all who kindly gave permission to include photos and quotes. Every effort has been made contact the copyright holder of every image and quoted text and to acknowledge them correctly. We apologize for any unintentional omissions or errors. They will be corrected in future editions of this book. Photos not otherwise credited come from the archives of Hibiscus and his family. The page numbers on which each image appears are listed below, along with the locator legend: (t=top, b=bottom, l=left, c=center, r=right).

Flower Power: Bernie Boston Archive, RIT Archive Collections: cover and 45; courtesy Wendy Fisher, 44; Pam Tent: 8, 72tl; W. Harris, 9; Kembrew McLeod: 10, 241; Ruth SoRelle: 34; James D. Gossage: 23t, 23b, 25, 31t, 31b; Dagmar: 28tc, 46; Robert Heide: 27r, John Gilman 27l; Dale Rose: 33, 207; David Hockney portrait: 36; Andrew Sherwood: 26, 28, 42, 105, 107, 137; Wendy Fisher: 45; Robert Altman: 50, 233; James Windsor, Tahara: 72tr, 248; Jerry Wainright 72bl; John Rothermel 72br; Ingeborg Gerdes: 64br, 75; Jilala (James Tressler): 57; Adrian Milton: 58, 60, 243; Robert Croonquist: 62l, 70, 235; Clay Geerdes: 72tl, 77; Lendon Sadler: 74; *Luminous Procuress:* film, 69, 86; Bud Lee: 71; Andrew Blauvelt: 74; Gregory Pickup: *Pickup's Tricks:* 78, 89; Fayette Hauser: 76, 238; Lee Mentley: 79; Joshua Freiwald: 80; David Wise: 82; Mary Ellen Mark: 85, Promo for *The Cockettes:* by David Weissman & Bill Weber, 2002: 71, 210; Allen Ginsberg: 95; William Frothingham (Palm Spareeeengz): 96, 97, 99, 100, 212; David Loehr: 109b, 113, 118; Peter Hujar: 110; Sheyla Bakyal: 106, 116, 125, 126tl, 126tr, 126lc, 126bl, 126br, 133, 134t; Patricia Harris: 116; Eloise Harris: 114; Do Lee: 120, 147; Marsha P. Johnson: 123; Dan Nicoletta: 124, 159, 160, 163, 164t, 164b; Shelley Valfer: 127; Ilka Scobie: 130; Charles Caron: 134b, 205, 228; Daily News: 140; Ritsaert ten Cate: 144; Agosto Machado: 146; Amron: 161; Irene Young: 178; Kenn Duncan: 181t; Don Marino: 181b; Dave Simmons: 182; R. Shay: 185; Geretta: 213; Steve Zehentner: 216, 234; Paul Zone: 193; Robert Tannanis: 194; Andrew Werner, 196; Charles Moniz, 198; Michael Ian: 206l, 227; Jim Bowers / Warner Brothers / CapedWonder.com, 206r, 231; Laurence Gartel: 218; Kenneth Ansloan: 224; Carol Dean: 219; Bobby Reed: 220; Curtis Bryant: 221; Timothy Bellavia: 222; Lauren: 235; Laurence Frommer: 236; Rumi Missabu, aka James Bartlett: 243; Martin Worman: 62r, 249

FOOTNOTES:

Cover Photo: Bernie Boston, courtesy Bernie Boston Collection, RIT Archive Collection; Becky Simmons, Archivist

How This Book Came To Be:
1. David Douglas Duncan, Bernie Boston, "The Vietnam Wars / 50 Years Ago -- Two Countries Torn Apart." Time Inc. Specials, LIFE Magazine, September 4, 2014, cover. Bernie Boston/RIT Archive Collections, Rochester Institute of Technology

Introduction: Pam Tent, founding member of The Cockettes, author of *Midnight at the Palace: my life as a fabulous Cockette.* Los Angeles, Alyson Books, 2004.

Chapter 1.
1. Peter Pan *written by J. M. Barrie, The song* Never Never Land:
 Music: Jule Styne, Lyrics: Comden and Green
2. Servicemen's Readjustment Act (G.I. Bill*)*
http://www.benefits.va.gov/gibill/history.asp
3. Walter Michael Harris*, Caravan to Oz: a family reinvents itself off-off-Broadway,* (New York-Seattle: El Dorado Books, August 2014). Pg. 23
4. The Clearwater Sun; *Unsinkable Titanic Triumph*;
review by Beverly Hutchins; October 19, 1962
5. Florida Sodomy Law - *http://www.hrc.org/laws-and-legislation/entry/florida-sodomy-law*

Chapter 2.
1. Drawing by David Hockney, British Artist, 1966. The inscription reads, "George in a fur coat. New York, Dec. '66."

Chapter 3.
1. David Kerry Heefner, *The Gorilla Was Gay: Remembering Ronald Tavel's "Gorilla Queen"* OutHistory,org
2. https://en.wikipedia.org/wiki/Flower_power;
AND - November 19: Allen Ginsberg invents "flower power"
– 1965 The Most Revolutionary Year in Music
3. Courtesy Bernie Boston Collection, RIT Archive Collection
4. Alice Ashe, Curio Magazine, James Madison University, 2005, pp. 11–14

Chapter 4.
1. Mark Thompson's profile of, and interview with, Hibiscus in his book, *Gay Spirit: Myth and Meaning*

252

2. The Nocturnal Dream Shows, Kaliflower and the Birth of The Cockettes, Martin Worman with Robert Croonquist, From *Midnight Masquerade*, unpublished dissertation of Martin Worman, 1992
3. Lendon Sadler, founding member of the Cockettes
5. Andrew Blauvelt, *Hippie Modernism - The Struggle for Utopia*, Walker Art Center, Minneapolis, MN; exhibit catalog (Pg. 288)

Chapter 5.
1. Fayette Hauser, *The Cockettes,* Interviewed by Maggie Kelly: *ODDA*, February 2016, Issue 10, Tributes
2. Michael Varrati, Interviewing Rumi Missabu – Cockette; and Italian horror icon Geretta, published on Peaches Christ's web site, "Drag Dossier #2," August 28, 2012. http://www.peacheschrist.com/
3. David Talbot, *Season of the Witch,* Chapter 12, The Palace Of Golden Cocks, Pgs. 100,104,105,106
4. Andrew Blauvelt, *Hippie Modernism - The Struggle for Utopia*, Walker Art Center, Minneapolis, MN; exhibit catalog

Chapter 6.
1. Michael Varrati, Interviewing Rumi Missabu – Cockette; and Italian horror icon Geretta, published on Peaches Christ's web site, "Drag Dossier #2," August 28, 2012. http://www.peacheschrist.com/?p=9512
2. *New York Times Style* Section on November 9, 1971
Excerpt of: The Cockettes: The Show Was a Drag
3. John Edward Heys, interview from *BOMB* magazine
4. *After Dark*, On High with the Angels of Light
    Excerpt by Henry Edwards, August 1973
5. Tim Robbins, *Caravan to Oz, a family reinvents itself off-off-Broadway*, El Dorado Books USA, 2014 *(pg. 141)*
6. Marsha P. Johnson, https://en.wikipedia.org/wiki/Marsha_P._Johnson
7. http://www.ranker.com
8. Tim Robbins, *Caravan to Oz, a family reinvents itself off-off-Broadway*, El Dorado Books USA, 2014, pg. 136

Chapter 7.
1. Actuel Magazine #38 cover, 4 Jan. 1974, courtesy Skot Herrin
2. Photo of The Angels of Light at the film premiere of *Ladies and Gentlemen, The Rolling Stones*, Ziegfeld Theatre, New York, 1974.
3. François Weyergans, Bejart Film

Part IV – The Finale
1. *The New York Times, Style Section, Karma Chameleon by Horacio Silva,* *2003*

Chapter 10.
1. Poster art by Dave Simmons, Hollywood Art Service, NYC, 1981
2. Laurence Frommer, cast member of *Hibiscus,* a musical co-written by W. Michael Harris, Rebecca Stone and Vida Mida Benjamin, with music by Ann Harris, Frederic Harris and Daniel Barry, presented by Ellen Stewart at La Mama ETC, NYC, 1992
3. Topman Magazine: *Hibiscus Glitters the Lily,* Photos by Irene Young, circa 1982
4. Lance Loud played the eldest son on *An American Family,* an early reality TV show, which premiered on PBS in 1973. http://www.pbs.org/lanceloud

Chapter 11.
1. Ann Harris, *Caravan to Oz, a family reinvents itself off-off-Broadway,* El Dorado Books USA, 2014, pg. 183, www.caravantooz.com
2. Michael's Thing magazine, Screaming Violets Remember Hibiscus, 1982

ENCORE! - One Rhinestone - A Thousand Ripples
1. Gleiberman, Entertainment Weekly, 10 Jul 2002
2. Kenneth Turan, Los Angeles Times, 26 Jul 2002
3. Holly Woodlawn, *The Holly Woodlawn Story, A Low Life in High Heels* with Jeff Copeland – Introduction by Paul Morrissey, *1991*
4. Michael Varrati, interviewing Rumi Missabu - Cockette - reprinted from Peaches Christ's Drag Dossier #2 www.peacheschrist.com

254

Appendix 1

Hibiscus' life and legacy are celebrated through film, literature, fashion and art:

1) *Caffe Cino and its Legacy*, a ten-week exhibit at the Vincent Astor Gallery of the New York Public Library for the Performing Arts at Lincoln Center, 1985

2) *Hibiscus, the musical* – Pilgrim Center for the Arts, Seattle, WA (1992)

3) *Hibiscus, the musical* – La MaMa ETC, NYC (1994)

4) *The Cockettes Are Coming*! Performance event at Theater for the New City

5) David Weissman and Bill Weber created a feature length documentary, <u>The Cockettes</u> (2002): *Official Sundance Film Festival Selection*; *Winner of the LA Film Critics Award for BEST DOCUMENTARY of 2002.*

6) *The Coffeehouse Chronicles*, spotlight on The Harris Family – La MaMa, 2005

7) Celebrating donation of the <u>Martin Worman Papers</u> to the New York Public Library for the Performing Arts, Billy Rose Theater Division at Lincoln Center, New York City, 2008

8) "Karma Chameleon" - *The New York Times Magazine* – Horacio Silva, 2003

9) *Last Address* - a film and exhibitions eulogizing a generation of New York City artists who died of AIDS, by the New York-based, filmmakers Ira Sachs and Lynne Sachs. (2010) www.lastaddress.org

Last Address uses photographs of the exteriors of the houses, apartment buildings, and lofts where 18 of these artists— Patrick Angus, Reinaldo Arenas, John D. Brockmeyer, Howard Brookner, Ethyl Eichelberger, Felix Gonzalez-Torres, Keith Haring, Hibiscus, Peter Hujar, Harry Kondoleon, Charles Ludlam, Jim Lyons, Robert Mapplethorpe, Cookie Mueller, Vito Russo, Assotto Saint, Ron Vawter, and David Wojnarowicz—were living at the time of their deaths to mark the disappearance of a generation.

10) Museum of Contemporary Art, Denver, CO, plus touring exhibit, 2012-2013

11) *West of Center: Art and the Counterculture Experiment in America,* 1965-1977 - February 09, 2013 to April 28, 2013:

12) *LIFE Magazine*: "The Vietnam Wars / 50 Years Ago - Two Countries Torn Apart." (2014)

13) *Hippie Modernism – The Struggle for Utopia* by Andrew Blauvelt and Greg Castillo, Walker Art Center, 2015

14) Celebrating donation of the Rumi Missabu - Cockettes/Gay Theater Archives to the New York Public Library for the Performing Arts, Billy Rose Theater Division at Lincoln Center, NYC, 2016

15) Michael Cepress', *Counter-Couture: Fashioning Identity in the American Counterculture,* September 2015 – January 2016, Bellevue Arts Museum, Bellevue, WA; and Museum of Arts and Design, New York City, March-August 2017.

Counter-Couture celebrates the handmade fashion and style of the 1960s and 1970s. Often referred to as the hippie movement, the Counterculture of the era swept away the conformism of the previous decade and professed an alternative lifestyle whose effects still resonate today. http://michaelcepress.com/home/

16) Visual AIDS Walk - Starting with a screening of Ira Sachs' film *Last Address* - Visual AIDS Programs Director Alex Fialho led a tribute walk honoring artists who lived with HIV / were lost to AIDS: Marsha P. Johnson, Barton Lidice Benes, Charles Ludlam, Cookie Mueller, Hibiscus, Ron Vawter. The life of their work continues to address, inspire, and live with a new generation today.

256

Appendix 2

George Harris III aka Hibiscus' Career
Member of: Actors Equity Association
Screen Actors Guild, American Guild of Variety Artists
American Federation of Television and Radio Artists

1962 – 64
THE EL DORADO PLAYERS in Clearwater, Florida:
Bluebeard, The Sheep and the Cheapskate, Camelot, Cleopatra, Queen of the Nile; The Unsinkable Titanic (film)

IMPROV
The Madcaps, Clearwater, Florida

FRANCIS WILSON PLAYHOUSE: Clearwater Florida
The Nuremburg Stove
Mrs. McThing
Hop O' My Thumb

1965-1967
BROADWAY
The Porcelain Year (Fred) - 1965

OFF BROADWAY
The Little Birds Fly (Philippe) by Harding Lemay, 1965
The Peace Creeps (John Wallace) by John Wolfson, 1966
Gorilla Queen (Glitz) by Ron Tavel, 1967
Sky High (new version) – Entermedia Theater NYC - 1979
Sky High (new version) – Players Theater NYC - 1979
Tinsel Town Tirade - Theater for the New City NYC - 1982

OFF-OFF-BROADWAY
Café Cino:
A Funny Walk Home by Jeff Weiss, 1967
Springtime Extravaganza (Himself)

La MaMa ETC, Young Playwrights Series, New York
The El Dorado Players: (Wrote, Directed, Performed, Produced)
Bluebeard by Ann Harris, 1965
The Sheep and the Cheapskate by Ann Harris, 1965
MacBee by Ann, George and Walter Harris, 1966
There is Method in their Madness by Ann, George and Walter Harris

257

Judson Poets Theater:
THE EL DORADO PLAYERS (Wrote, Directed, Performed)
The Sheep and the Cheapskate by Ann Harris, 1965
Remember the Thirties (Gary Cooper) 1965
Sing Ho! for a Bear (Rabbit) adapted from A. A. Milne, music by Al
Carmines, 1964

COMMUNITY THEATER, TOURING & SUMMER STOCK
Papermill Playhouse; Westport; Sharon Tappan Zee; Bucks County
Playhouse; Lead performer with Dolphin Players; Orange Blossom
Playhouse Orlando, Florida; Francis Wilson Playhouse and Coconut Grove
Playhouse, Florida with the Jesters in *King Lear, Macbeth & Romeo and
Juliet.*

1969-1979
THE COCKETTES in San Francisco, founded by Hibiscus:
*Palace Theater debut; Blue Angel Cabaret; Cotton Club Cabaret,
Earthquake; Gone with The Showboat To Oklahoma; Paste on Paste;
Fairytale Extravaganza; Hollywood Babylon; Hot Voo Doo; Myth Thing;
Les Cockettes de Paree; Pearls Over Shanghai, Les Ghouls, Tinsel Tarts in a
Hot Coma, Madame Butterfly Grace Cathedral-Christmas show, Morrocan
Opera, Polk Street Fair*

THE ANGELS OF LIGHT
(Founder, Writer, Director, Performer)
Birdie Follies – Westbeth, NYC
Sky High - Westbeth, NYC
Enchanted Miracle – Theater for the New City, NYC
Gossamer Wings – Theater for the New City, NYC
Razzamatazz – Theater for the New City, NYC
The Shocking Pink Life of Jayne Champagne - Players Theater, San
Francisco

EUROPE - THE ANGELS OF LIGHT
(Wrote, Directed, Performed, Produced)
Enchanted Miracle – The Roundhouse, London, England
Enchanted Miracle – Theater 160, Brussels, Belgium
Enchanted Miracle – Holland Festival
Razzamatazz - Mickery Theater, Amsterdam, Holland
Razzamatazz - Nancy France Theatre Festival du Mondial, *Razzamatazz* -
Akademie Der Kunste, Berlin, Germany
Razzamatazz – Theater Campaign Premiere, Paris, France
Potel et Chabot for Mazda – Paris, France

FEATURE FILMS & DOCUMENTARIES
I Was Born in Venice – Cannes Film Festival 1976
Luminous Procuress – dir. Steven Arnold, San Francisco 1971
Elevator Girls in Bondage – dir. Michael Kalmen, San Francisco 1972
Angels of Light, dir Mary Jordan (unreleased work in progress)
The Cockettes, dir Bill Weber and David Weissman, 2002
Last Address, a film by Ira Sachs, 2010
Pickup's Tricks, director Gregory Pickup, 1973
Life of Bejart, director François Weyergans, Brussels

FEATURE VIDEO FOR TELEVISION AND NEWS MEDIA
Film for French TV of 1975 Festival Mondial du Theatre, Nancy (the Angels of Light took top honors at this festival)

TELEVISION COMMERCIALS & VOICEOVERS
The Madcaps, Radio in Clearwater, Florida, 1960-1963
Patty Duke Show
Shirley Clarke, Channel 13 Special - 1973
Mazda Car & Light Co. (Paris) -1975
Angels of Light – Amsterdam TV Special -1975
Edge of Night, (Waiter) CBS Soap Opera - 1980-1982

HIBISCUS AND THE SCREAMING VIOLETS
 (NYC music clubs); 1018; Studio 54; CBGB; The Ballroom; The Bitter End; BONDS; Copacabana; Danceteria; Earth Day Festival (Catskills); Eighty Eights; Gildersleeves; The Ice Palace, Fire Island & Ice Palace, NYC; The Limelight; Magique Club; Malibu Club; The Mudd Club; Peppermint Lounge; Opened for Buster Poindexter; The Roxy; The Reggae Lounge; RT Firefly; SNAFU; Theater for the New City Halloween

BROADCAST MEDIA INTERVIEWS
Lifestyles of the Rich & Famous - Robin Leach interviews Hibiscus and the Screaming Violets

PRINT MEDIA PROFILES & INTERVIEWS
"At Home With Hibiscus" -The San Francisco Oracle, 1968
The Berkeley Barb's coverage of The Cockettes, 1968-1970
"Les Cockettes," Rolling Stone #93 –1971
Press coverage of The El Dorado Players in Florida and New York; The Cockettes in San Francisco; The Angels of Light in New York and Europe; Hibiscus and the Screaming Violets and The Harris Sisters in New York, Pilgrim Center for the Arts in Seattle.

BOOKS

Adler, Richard, and Lee Davis. *You Gotta Have Heart.* New York: D.I. Fine, 1990.

Auther, Elissa and Lerner, Adam, ed. *West of Center: art and the counterculture experiment in america,* 1965-1977. Minneapolis: University Of Minnesota Press, 2011.

Berger, Dan. *The Hidden 1970s: histories of radicalism.* New Brunswick: Rutgers University Press, 2010.

Bottoms, Stephen. *The Sixties, Center Stage, mainstream and popular performances in a turbulent decade.* Edited by James M. Harding and Cindy Rosenthal. Ann Arbor: University of Michigan Press, 2017

Brooks, Adrian and Daniel Nicoletta, *Flights of Angels.* Vancouver: Los Angeles: The Pop Underground.

Crespy, David Allison. *Off-Off-Broadway Explosion: how provocative playwrights of the 1960s ignited a new American theater.* New York: Back Stage Books, 2003.

Dominic, Magie, and Smith, Michael, ed. H.M. Koutoukas 1937–2010, remembered by his friends. Silverton: Fast Books, 2010.

Gamson, Joshua. *The Fabulous Sylvester: the legend, the music, the seventies in San Francisco.* New York: Henry Holt & Company, 2005. 302 Running Press, 2010.

Gruen, John. *The New Bohemia.* New York: Shorecrest, Inc., 1966.

Haden -Guest, Anthony, and Niels Kummer; Felice Quinto; Domitilla Sartogo; et al. *Studio 54: The Legend.* New York: teNeues, 1997.

Harris, Ann, with Walter Michael Harris, Jayne Anne Harris-Kelley, Eloise Harris-Damone, Mary Lou Harris-Pietsch. *Caravan to Oz – a family reinvents itself off-off-broadway.* New York: El Dorado Books USA, 2014

Heide, Robert, and John Gilman. Greenwich Village: a primo guide to shopping, eating, and making merry in true Bohemia. New York: St. Martins Griffin ed., 1995. Robert Heide's *25 Plays* will be released in Fall 2017 by Fast Books. For more information, visit www.fastbookspress.com

Kolsbun, Ken, and Michael Sweeny. *Peace: the biography of a symbol.* Washington, D.C.: National Geographic, 2008.

Lake, Bambi, and Alvin Orloff. *The Unsinkable Bambi Lake: a fairy tale containing the dish on Cockettes, punks & angels.* San Francisco: Manic D Press, 1996.

Lucas, Phillip. *The Odyssey of a New Religion: the Holy Order of MANS from new age to orthodoxy.* Bloomington: Indiana University Press, 1995.

Macleod, Kembrew. *The Pop Underground*, a forthcoming book to be published by Abrams in fall 2018

Mulligan, Therese. *Bernie Boston, american photojournalist.* Rochester, New York: RIT Cary Graphic Arts Press, 2002

Rose, Susan Dale. *Upon Our Westward Way:* Myron Coloney, Josephine Artemisia Coloney, and an american adventure. Lexington: Blue Horse Books, 2012.

Smith, Michael, ed. *The Best of Off-Off-Broadway.* New York: E.P. Dutton Inc., 1969.

Stone, Wendell. *Caffe Cino: the birthplace of off-off-Broadway.* Carbondale: Southern Illinois University Press, 2005.

Susoyev, Steve and George Birimisa. *Return to the Caffe Cino.* San Francisco: Moving Finger Press, 2007.

Talbot, David. *Season of the Witch,* Free Press (a division of Simon & Schuster Inc., 2012.

Tent, Pam. M*idnight at the Palace: my life as a fabulous Cockette.* Los Angeles: Alyson Books, 2004.

Thompson, Mark. *Gay Spirit - myth and meaning.* New York: St. Martin's Press, 1987.

Trinidad, David. Plasticville - poems. London: Turnaround, 2000.

Woodlawn, Holly. *A Low Life in High Heels.* New York: St. Martins Press. 1991.

Appendix 3

Links and Resources
For additional content and news, please visit:

Flower Power photo by Bernie Boston
https://web.archive.org/web/20090920062711/http://www.curiomagazine.co
m/archives/2005/images/boston.pdf

Flower Power Man: www.flowerpowerman.com
Caravan to Oz web site and blog: www.caravantooz.com

They Acted Everywhere:
The Harris Family on Robert Patrick's Cino Pages
http://caffecino.wordpress.com/1938/01/01/harris-family/

Caffe Cino: Robert Patrick's Cino Pages
http://caffecino.wordpress.com/

The Cockettes (2002 documentary film by co-directed by
David Weissman and Bill Weber) http://www.cockettes.com/

Gorilla Queen remembered: David Kerry Heefner's reflections on a much
loved off-off-Broadway play of the 1960s. (see Part II for G3)
http://outhistory.org/exhibits/showiththe-gorilla-was-gay/part-i
http://outhistory.org/exhibits/showiththe-gorilla-was-gay/part-ii

The Billy Rose Theatre Collection
http://www.nypl.org/find-archival-materials
Caffe Cino / Joe Cino Collection / Magie Dominic Collection
James D. Gossage Collection / Circle Theater Collection

HAIR (the musical)
http://www.michaelbutler.com/hair/holding/Hair.html

Dagmar Krajnc, HAIR's photographer: www.dagmarfoto.com

George E. Harris, Sr. – essay by Walter Michael Harris
http://www.capedwonder.com/george-harris-officer-mooney/

La MaMa Experimental Theater Club, NYC
http://lamama.org/

Pickup's Tricks, a 1973 film by Gregory Pickup featuring Hibiscus, the Cockettes, Allen Ginsberg and the San Francisco Angels of Light: www.pickupstricks.com

Studio 54: http://en.wikipedia.org/wiki/Studio_54

Theater for the New City
http://www.theaterforthenewcity.net

With love to all of our friends
Here and in paradise,
The Harris Family

EL DORADO
B O O K S
USA

NEW YORK – SEATTLE
FlowerPowerMan.com

Made in the USA
Columbia, SC
22 October 2017